STIGMA
NOTES ON THE MANAGEMENT OF SPOILED IDENTITY

by Erving Goffman

A TOUCHSTONE BOOK
Published by Simon & Schuster Inc.
New York London Toronto

Copyright © 1963 by Simon & Schuster, Inc.

All rights reserved
including the right of reproduction
in whole or in part in any form

First Touchstone Edition, 1986

Published by Simon & Schuster, Inc.

Rockefeller Center
1230 Avenue of the Americas
New York, New York 10020

Originally published by Prentice-Hall, Inc.

TOUCHSTONE and colophon are registered trademarks of
Simon & Schuster, Inc.

Manufactured in the United States of America

40 39 38 37 36 35 34 33 32 31   Pbk.

Library of Congress Cataloging-in-Publication Data

Goffman, Erving.
  Stigma: notes on the management of spoiled identity.

  Includes bibliographical references.
  1. Stigma (Social psychology)   2. Identity (Psychology)
I. Title.
HM291.G624   1986   155.2   84-46153
ISBN 0-671-62244-7 Pbk.

PREFACE

For over a decade now in the literature of social psychology there has been good work done on stigma—the situation of the individual who is disqualified from full social acceptance.[1] This work has been added to from time to time by useful clinical studies,[2] and its framework applied to ever new categories of persons.[3]

In this essay[4] I want to review some work on stigma, especially some popular work, to see what it can yield for sociology. An exercise will be undertaken in marking off the material on stigma from neighboring facts, in showing how this material can be economically described within a single conceptual scheme, and in clarifying the relation of stigma to the subject matter of deviance. This task will allow me to formulate and use a special set of concepts, those that bear on "social information," the information the individual directly conveys about himself.

[1] Most notably, among sociologists, E. Lemert; among psychologists, K. Lewin, F. Heider, T. Dembo, R. Barker, and B. Wright. See especially B. Wright, *Physical Disability—A Psychological Approach* (New York: Harper & Row, 1960), which has provided me with many re-quotable quotations and many useful references.

[2] For example, F. Macgregor *et al.*, *Facial Deformities and Plastic Surgery* (Springfield, Ill.: Charles C Thomas, 1953).

[3] For example, C. Orbach, M. Bard, and A. Sutherland, "Fears and Defensive Adaptations to the Loss of Anal Sphincter Control," *Psychoanalytical Review*, XLIV (1957), 121-175.

[4] An earlier summary version is printed in M. Greenblatt, D Levinson, and R. Williams, *The Patient and the Mental Hospital* (New York: Free Press of Glencoe, 1957), pp. 507-510. A later version was presented at the MacIver Lecture at the Southern Sociological Society, Louisville, Kentucky, April 13, 1962. Assistance with the current version was received from the Center for the Study of Law and Society, University of California, Berkeley, under a grant from the President's Committee on Juvenile Delinquency.

CONTENTS

1. STIGMA AND SOCIAL IDENTITY . . . 1

   Preliminary Conceptions, 2; The Own and the Wise, 19; Moral Career, 32

2. INFORMATION CONTROL AND PERSONAL IDENTITY . . . 41

   The Discredited and the Discreditable, 41; Social Information, 43; Visibility, 48; Personal Identity, 51; Biography, 62; Biographical Others, 66; Passing, 73; Techniques of Information Control, 91; Covering, 102

3. GROUP ALIGNMENT AND EGO IDENTITY . . . 105

   Ambivalence, 106; Professional Presentations, 108; In-Group Alignments, 112; Out-Group Alignments, 114; The Politics of Identity, 123

4. THE SELF AND ITS OTHER . . . 126

   Deviations and Norms, 126; The Normal Deviant, 130; Stigma and Reality, 135

5. DEVIATIONS AND DEVIANCE . . . 140

Dear Miss Lonelyhearts—

I am sixteen years old now and I dont know what to do and would appreciate it if you could tell me what to do. When I was a little girl it was not so bad because I got used to the kids on the block makeing fun of me, but now I would like to have boy friends like the other girls and go out on Saturday nites, but no boy will take me because I was born without a nose—although I am a good dancer and have a nice shape and my father buys me pretty clothes.

I sit and look at myself all day and cry. I have a big hole in the middle of my face that scares people even myself so I cant blame the boys for not wanting to take me out. My mother loves me, but she crys terrible when she looks at me.

What did I do to deserve such a terrible bad fate? Even if I did do some bad things I didn't do any before I was a year old and I was born this way. I asked Papa and he says he doesnt know, but that maybe I did something in the other world before I was born or that maybe I was being punished for his sins. I dont believe that because he is a very nice man. Ought I commit suicide?

Sincerely yours,
Desperate

From *Miss Lonelyhearts* by Nathanael West, pp. 14-15. Copyright © 1962 by New Directions. Reprinted by permission of New Directions, Publishers.

1. STIGMA and SOCIAL IDENTITY

The Greeks, who were apparently strong on visual aids, originated the term *stigma* to refer to bodily signs designed to expose something unusual and bad about the moral status of the signifier. The signs were cut or burnt into the body and advertised that the bearer was a slave, a criminal, or a traitor—a blemished person, ritually polluted, to be avoided, especially in public places. Later, in Christian times, two layers of metaphor were added to the term: the first referred to bodily signs of holy grace that took the form of eruptive blossoms on the skin; the second, a medical allusion to this religious allusion, referred to bodily signs of physical disorder. Today the term is widely used in something like the original literal sense, but is applied more to the disgrace itself than to the bodily evidence of it. Furthermore, shifts have occurred in the kinds of disgrace that arouse concern. Students, however, have made little effort to describe the structural preconditions of stigma, or even to provide a definition of the concept itself. It seems necessary, therefore, to try at the beginning to sketch in some very general assumptions and definitions.

Preliminary Conceptions

Society establishes the means of categorizing persons and the complement of attributes felt to be ordinary and natural for members of each of these categories. Social settings establish the categories of persons likely to be encountered there. The routines of social intercourse in established settings allow us to deal with anticipated others without special attention or thought. When a stranger comes into our presence, then, first appearances are likely to enable us to anticipate his category and attributes, his "social identity"—to use a term that is better than "social status" because personal attributes such as "honesty" are involved, as well as structural ones, like "occupation."

We lean on these anticipations that we have, transforming them into normative expectations, into righteously presented demands.

Typically, we do not become aware that we have made these demands or aware of what they are until an active question arises as to whether or not they will be fulfilled. It is then that we are likely to realize that all along we had been making certain assumptions as to what the individual before us ought to be. Thus, the demands we make might better be called demands made "in effect," and the character we impute to the individual might better be seen as an imputation made in potential retrospect—a characterization "in effect," a *virtual social identity*. The category and attributes he could in fact be proved to possess will be called his *actual social identity*.

While the stranger is present before us, evidence can arise of his possessing an attribute that makes him different from others in the category of persons available for him to be, and of a less desirable kind—in the extreme, a person who is quite thoroughly bad, or dangerous, or weak. He is thus reduced in our minds from a whole and usual person to a tainted, discounted one. Such an attribute is a stigma, especially when its discrediting effect is very extensive; sometimes it is also called a failing, a shortcoming, a handicap. It constitutes a special discrepancy between virtual and actual social identity. Note that there are other types of discrepancy between virtual and actual social identity, for example the kind that causes us to reclassify an individual from one socially anticipated category to a different but equally well-anticipated one, and the kind that causes us to alter our estimation of the individual upward. Note, too, that not all undesirable attributes are at issue, but only those which are incongruous with our stereotype of what a given type of individual should be.

The term stigma, then, will be used to refer to an attribute that is deeply discrediting, but it should be seen that a language of relationships, not attributes, is really needed. An attribute that stigmatizes one type of possessor can confirm the usualness of another, and therefore is neither creditable nor discreditable as a thing in itself. For example, some jobs in America cause holders without the expected college education to conceal this fact; other jobs, however, can lead the few of their holders who have a higher education to keep this a secret, lest they be marked as failures and outsiders. Similarly, a middle class boy may feel no compunction in being seen going to the library; a professional criminal, however, writes:

> I can remember before now on more than one occasion, for instance, going into a public library near where I was living, and looking over my shoulder a couple of times before I actually went in just to make sure no one who knew me was standing about and seeing me do it.[1]

[1] T. Parker and R. Allerton, *The Courage of His Convictions* (London: Hutchinson & Co., 1962), p. 109.

So, too, an individual who desires to fight for his country may conceal a physical defect, lest his claimed physical status be discredited; later, the same individual, embittered and trying to get out of the army, may succeed in gaining admission to the army hospital, where he would be discredited if discovered in not really having an acute sickness.[2] A stigma, then, is really a special kind of relationship between attribute and stereotype, although I don't propose to continue to say so, in part because there are important attributes that almost everywhere in our society are discrediting.

The term stigma and its synonyms conceal a double perspective: does the stigmatized individual assume his differentness is known about already or is evident on the spot, or does he assume it is neither known about by those present nor immediately perceivable by them? In the first case one deals with the plight of the *discredited*, in the second with that of the *discreditable*. This is an important difference, even though a particular stigmatized individual is likely to have experience with both situations. I will begin with the situation of the discredited and move on to the discreditable but not always separate the two.

Three grossly different types of stigma may be mentioned. First there are abominations of the body—the various physical deformities. Next there are blemishes of individual character perceived as weak will, domineering or unnatural passions, treacherous and rigid beliefs, and dishonesty, these being inferred from a known record of, for example, mental disorder, imprisonment, addiction, alcoholism, homosexuality, unemployment, suicidal attempts, and radical political behavior. Finally there are the tribal stigma of race, nation, and religion, these being stigma that can be transmitted through lineages and equally contaminate all members of a family.[3] In all of these

---

[2] In this connection see the review by M. Meltzer, "Countermanipulation through Malingering," in A. Biderman and H. Zimmer, eds., *The Manipulation of Human Behavior* (New York: John Wiley & Sons, 1961), pp. 277-304.

[3] In recent history, especially in Britain, low class status functioned as an important tribal stigma, the sins of the parents, or at least their milieu, being visited

various instances of stigma, however, including those the Greeks had in mind, the same sociological features are found: an individual who might have been received easily in ordinary social intercourse possesses a trait that can obtrude itself upon attention and turn those of us whom he meets away from him, breaking the claim that his other attributes have on us. He possesses a stigma, an undesired differentness from what we had anticipated. We and those who do not depart negatively from the particular expectations at issue I shall call the *normals*.

The attitudes we normals have toward a person with a stigma, and the actions we take in regard to him, are well known, since these responses are what benevolent social action is designed to soften and ameliorate. By definition, of course, we believe the person with a stigma is not quite human. On this assumption we exercise varieties of discrimination, through which we effectively, if often unthinkingly, reduce his life chances. We construct a stigma-theory, an ideology to explain his inferiority and account for the danger he represents, sometimes rationalizing an animosity based on other differences, such as those of social class.[4] We use specific stigma terms such as cripple, bastard, moron in our daily discourse as a source of metaphor and imagery, typically without giving thought to the original meaning.[5] We tend to impute a wide range of imperfections on the basis of the original one,[6] and at the same time to impute some desirable but undesired attributes, often of a supernatural cast, such as "sixth sense," or "understanding":[7]

---

on the child, should the child rise improperly far above his initial station. The management of class stigma is of course a central theme in the English novel.

[4] D. Riesman, "Some Observations Concerning Marginality," *Phylon*, Second Quarter, 1951, 122.

[5] The case regarding mental patients is presented by T. J. Scheff in a forthcoming paper.

[6] In regard to the blind, see E. Henrich and L. Kriegel, eds., *Experiments in Survival* (New York: Association for the Aid of Crippled Children, 1961), pp. 152 and 186; and H. Chevigny, *My Eyes Have a Cold Nose* (New Haven, Conn.: Yale University Press, paperbound, 1962), p. 201.

[7] In the words of one blind woman, "I was asked to endorse a perfume, presumably because being sightless my sense of smell was super-discriminating." See T. Keitlen (with N. Lobsenz), *Farewell to Fear* (New York: Avon, 1962), p. 10.

For some, there may be a hesitancy about touching or steering the blind, while for others, the perceived failure to see may be generalized into a gestalt of disability, so that the individual shouts at the blind as if they were deaf or attempts to lift them as if they were crippled. Those confronting the blind may have a whole range of belief that is anchored in the stereotype. For instance, they may think they are subject to unique judgment, assuming the blinded individual draws on special channels of information unavailable to others.[8]

Further, we may perceive his defensive response to his situation as a direct expression of his defect, and then see both defect and response as just retribution for something he or his parents or his tribe did, and hence a justification of the way we treat him.[9]

Now turn from the normal to the person he is normal against. It seems generally true that members of a social category may strongly support a standard of judgment that they and others agree does not directly apply to them. Thus it is that a businessman may demand womanly behavior from females or ascetic behavior from monks, and not construe himself as someone who ought to realize either of these styles of conduct. The distinction is between realizing a norm and merely supporting it. The issue of stigma does not arise here, but only where there is some expectation on all sides that those in a given category should not only support a particular norm but also realize it.

Also, it seems possible for an individual to fail to live up to what we effectively demand of him, and yet be relatively untouched by this failure; insulated by his alienation, protected by identity beliefs of his own, he feels that he is a full-fledged normal human being, and that we are the ones who are not quite human. He bears a stigma but does not seem to be impressed or repentant about doing so. This possibility is celebrated in exemplary tales about Mennonites, Gypsies, shameless scoundrels, and very orthodox Jews.

[8] A. G. Gowman, *The War Blind in American Social Structure* (New York: American Foundation for the Blind, 1957), p. 198.
[9] For examples, see Macgregor *et al.*, *op. cit.*, throughout

STIGMA AND SOCIAL IDENTITY

In America at present, however, separate systems of honor seem to be on the decline. The stigmatized individual tends to hold the same beliefs about identity that we do; this is a pivotal fact. His deepest feelings about what he is may be his sense of being a "normal person," a human being like anyone else, a person, therefore, who deserves a fair chance and a fair break.[10] (Actually, however phrased, he bases his claims not on what he thinks is due *everyone*, but only everyone of a selected social category into which he unquestionably fits, for example, anyone of his age, sex, profession, and so forth.) Yet he may perceive, usually quite correctly, that whatever others profess, they do not really "accept" him and are not ready to make contact with him on "equal grounds."[11] Further, the standards he has incorporated from the wider society equip him to be intimately alive to what others see as his failing, inevitably causing him, if only for moments, to agree that he does indeed fall short of what he really ought to be. Shame becomes a central possibility, arising from the individual's perception of one of his own attributes as being a defiling thing to possess, and one he can readily see himself as not possessing.

The immediate presence of normals is likely to reinforce this split between self-demands and self, but in fact self-hate and self-derogation can also occur when only he and a mirror are about:

> When I got up at last . . . and had learned to walk again, one day I took a hand glass and went to a long mirror to look at myself, and I went alone. I didn't want anyone . . . to know how I felt when I saw myself for the first time. But there was no noise, no out-

[10] The notion of "normal human being" may have its source in the medical approach to humanity or in the tendency of large-scale bureaucratic organizations, such as the nation state, to treat all members in some respects as equal. Whatever its origins, it seems to provide the basic imagery through which laymen currently conceive of themselves. Interestingly, a convention seems to have emerged in popular life-story writing where a questionable person proves his claim to normalcy by citing his acquisition of a spouse and children, and, oddly, by attesting to his spending Christmas and Thanksgiving with them.

[11] A criminal's view of this nonacceptance is presented in Parker and Allerton, *op. cit.*, pp. 110-111.

cry; I didn't scream with rage when I saw myself. I just felt numb. That person in the mirror *couldn't* be me. I felt inside like a healthy, ordinary, lucky person—oh, not like the one in the mirror! Yet when I turned my face to the mirror there were my own eyes looking back, hot with shame . . . when I did not cry or make any sound, it became impossible that I should speak of it to anyone, and the confusion and the panic of my discovery were locked inside me then and there, to be faced alone, for a very long time to come.[12]

Over and over I forgot what I had seen in the mirror. It could not penetrate into the interior of my mind and become an integral part of me. I felt as if it had nothing to do with me; it was only a disguise. But it was not the kind of disguise which is put on voluntarily by the person who wears it, and which is intended to confuse other people as to one's identity. My disguise had been put on me without my consent or knowledge like the ones in fairy tales, and it was I myself who was confused by it, as to my own identity. I looked in the mirror, and was horror-struck because I did not recognize myself. In the place where I was standing, with that persistent romantic elation in me, as if I were a favored fortunate person to whom everything was possible, I saw a stranger, a little, pitiable, hideous figure, and a face that became, as I stared at it, painful and blushing with shame. It was only a disguise, but it was on me, for life. It was there, it was there, it was real. Every one of those encounters was like a blow on the head. They left me dazed and dumb and senseless everytime, until slowly and stubbornly my robust persistent illusion of well-being and of personal beauty spread all through me again, and I forgot the irrelevant reality and was all unprepared and vulnerable again.[13]

The central feature of the stigmatized individual's situation in life can now be stated. It is a question of what is often, if vaguely, called "acceptance." Those who have dealings with him fail to accord him the respect and regard which the un-

[12] K. B. Hathaway, *The Little Locksmith* (New York: Coward-McCann, 1943), p. 41, in Wright, *op. cit.*, p. 157.

[13] *Ibid.*, pp. 46-47. For general treatments of the self-disliking sentiments, see K. Lewin, *Resolving Social Conflicts*, Part III (New York: Harper & Row, 1948); A. Kardiner and L. Ovesey, *The Mark of Oppression: A Psychosocial Study of the American Negro* (New York: W. W. Norton & Company, 1951); and E. H. Erikson, *Childhood and Society* (New York: W. W. Norton & Company, 1950).

contaminated aspects of his social identity have led them to anticipate extending, and have led him to a... ...pate receiving; he echoes this denial by finding that some of his own attributes warrant it.

How does the stigmatized person respond to his situation? In some cases it will be possible for him to make a direct attempt to correct what he sees as the objective basis of his failing, as when a physically deformed person undergoes plastic surgery, a blind person eye treatment, an illiterate remedial education, a homosexual psychotherapy. (Where such repair is possible, what often results is not the acquisition of fully normal status, but a transformation of self from someone with a particular blemish into someone with a record of having corrected a particular blemish.) Here proneness to "victimization" is to be cited, a result of the stigmatized person's exposure to fraudulent servers selling speech correction, skin lighteners, body stretchers, youth restorers (as in rejuvenation through fertilized egg yolk treatment), cures through faith, and poise in conversation. Whether a practical technique or fraud is involved, the quest, often secret, that results provides a special indication of the extremes to which the stigmatized can be willing to go, and hence the painfulness of the situation that leads them to these extremes. One illustration may be cited:

> Miss Peck [a pioneer New York social worker for the hard of hearing] said that in the early days the quacks and get-rich-quick medicine men who abounded saw the League [for the hard of hearing] as their happy hunting ground, ideal for the promotion of magnetic head caps, miraculous vibrating machines, artificial eardrums, blowers, inhalers, massagers, magic oils, balsams, and other guaranteed, sure-fire, positive, and permanent cure-alls for incurable deafness. Advertisements for such hokum (until the 1920's when the American Medical Association moved in with an investigation campaign) beset the hard of hearing in the pages of the daily press, even in reputable magazines.[14]

[14] F. Warfield, *Keep Listening* (New York: The Viking Press, 1957), p. 76. See also H. von Hentig, *The Criminal and His Victim* (New Haven, Conn.: Yale University Press, 1948), p. 101.

The stigmatized individual can also attempt to correct his condition indirectly by devoting much private effort to the mastery of areas of activity ordinarily felt to be closed on incidental and physical grounds to one with his shortcoming. This is illustrated by the lame person who learns or re-learns to swim, ride, play tennis, or fly an airplane, or the blind person who becomes expert at skiing and mountain climbing.[15] Tortured learning may be associated, of course, with the tortured performance of what is learned, as when an individual, confined to a wheelchair, manages to take to the dance floor with a girl in some kind of mimicry of dancing.[16] Finally, the person with a shameful differentness can break with what is called reality, and obstinately attempt to employ an unconventional interpretation of the character of his social identity.

The stigmatized individual is likely to use his stigma for "secondary gains," as an excuse for ill success that has come his way for other reasons:

> For years the scar, harelip or misshapen nose has been looked on as a handicap, and its importance in the social and emotional adjustment is unconsciously all embracing. It is the "hook" on which the patient has hung all inadequacies, all dissatisfactions, all procrastinations and all unpleasant duties of social life, and he has come to depend on it not only as a reasonable escape from competition but as a protection from social responsibility.
>
> When one removes this factor by surgical repair, the patient is cast adrift from the more or less acceptable emotional protection it has offered and soon he finds, to his surprise and discomfort, that life is not all smooth sailing even for those with unblemished, "ordinary" faces. He is unprepared to cope with this situation without the support of a "handicap," and he may turn to the less simple, but similar, protection of the behavior patterns of neurasthenia, hysterical conversion, hypochondriasis or the acute anxiety states.[17]

---

[15] Keitlen, *op. cit.*, Chap. 12, pp. 117-129 and Chap. 14, pp. 137-149. See also Chevigny, *op. cit.*, pp. 85-86.

[16] Henrich and Kriegel, *op. cit.*, p. 49.

[17] W. Y. Baker and L. H. Smith, "Facial Disfigurement and Personality," *Journal of the American Medical Association*, CXII (1939), 303. Macgregor *et al.*, *op. cit.*, p. 57 ff., provide an illustration of a man who used his big red nose for a crutch.

He may also see the trials he has suffered as a blessing in disguise, especially because of what it is felt that suffering can teach one about life and people:

> But now, far away from the hospital experience, I can evaluate what I have learned. [A mother permanently disabled by polio writes.] For it wasn't only suffering: it was also learning through suffering. I know my awareness of people has deepened and increased, that those who are close to me can count on me to turn all my mind and heart and attention to their problems. I could not have learned *that* dashing all over a tennis court.[18]

Correspondingly, he can come to re-assess the limitations of normals, as a multiple sclerotic suggests:

> Both healthy minds and healthy bodies may be crippled. The fact that "normal" people can get around, can see, can hear, doesn't mean that they are seeing or hearing. They can be very blind to the things that spoil their happiness, very deaf to the pleas of others for kindness; when I think of them I do not feel any more crippled or disabled than they. Perhaps in some small way I can be the means of opening their eyes to the beauties around us: things like a warm handclasp, a voice that is anxious to cheer, a spring breeze, music to listen to, a friendly nod. These people are important to me, and I like to feel that I can help them.[19]

And a blind writer.

> That would lead immediately to the thought that there are many occurrences which can diminish satisfaction in living far more effectively than blindness, and that lead would be an entirely healthy one to take. In this light, we can perceive, for instance, that some inadequacy like the inability to accept human love, which can effectively diminish satisfaction of living almost to the vanishing point, is far more a tragedy than blindness. But it is unusual for the man who suffers from such a malady even to know he has it and self pity is, therefore, impossible for him.[20]

[18] Henrich and Kriegel, *op. cit.*, p. 19.
[19] *Ibid.*, p. 35.
[20] Chevigny, *op. cit.*, p. 154.

And a cripple:

> As life went on, I learned of many, many different kinds of handicap, not only the physical ones, and I began to realize that the words of the crippled girl in the extract above [words of bitterness] could just as well have been spoken by young women who had never needed crutches, women who felt inferior and different because of ugliness, or inability to bear children, or helplessness in contacting people, or many other reasons.[21]

The responses of the normal and of the stigmatized that have been considered so far are ones which can occur over protracted periods of time and in isolation from current contact between normals and stigmatized.[22] This book, however, is specifically concerned with the issue of "mixed contacts"—the moments when stigmatized and normal are in the same "social situation," that is, in one another's immediate physical presence, whether in a conversation-like encounter or in the mere co-presence of an unfocused gathering.

The very anticipation of such contacts can of course lead normals and the stigmatized to arrange life so as to avoid them. Presumably this will have larger consequences for the stigmatized, since more arranging will usually be necessary on their part:

> Before her disfigurement [amputation of the distal half of her nose] Mrs. Dover, who lived with one of her two married daughters, had been an independent, warm and friendly woman who enjoyed traveling, shopping, and visiting her many relatives. The disfigurement of her face, however, resulted in a definite alteration in her way of living. The first two or three years she seldom left her daughter's home, preferring to remain in her room or to sit in the backyard. "I was heartsick," she said; "the door had been shut on my life."[23]

---

[21] F. Carling, *And Yet We Are Human* (London: Chatto & Windus, 1962), pp. 23-24.
[22] For one review, see G. W. Allport, *The Nature of Prejudice* (New York: Anchor Books, 1958).
[23] Macgregor *et al.*, *op. cit.*, pp. 91-92.

Lacking the salutary feed-back of daily social intercourse with others, the self-isolate can become suspicious, depressed, hostile, anxious, and bewildered. Sullivan's version may be cited:

> The awareness of inferiority means that one is unable to keep out of consciousness the formulation of some chronic feeling of the worst sort of insecurity, and this means that one suffers anxiety and perhaps even something worse, if jealousy is really worse than anxiety. The fear that others can disrespect a person because of something he shows means that he is always insecure in his contact with other people; and this insecurity arises, not from mysterious and somewhat disguised sources, as a great deal of our anxiety does, but from something which he knows he cannot fix. Now that represents an almost fatal deficiency of the self-system, since the self is unable to disguise or exclude a definite formulation that reads, "I am inferior. Therefore people will dislike me and I cannot be secure with them."[24]

When normals and stigmatized do in fact enter one another's immediate presence, especially when they there attempt to sustain a joint conversational encounter, there occurs one of the primal scenes of sociology; for, in many cases, these moments will be the ones when the causes and effects of stigma must be directly confronted by both sides.

The stigmatized individual may find that he feels unsure of how we normals will identify him and receive him.[25] An illustration may be cited from a student of physical disability:

> Uncertainty of status for the disabled person obtains over a wide range of social interactions in addition to that of employment. The blind, the ill, the deaf, the crippled can never be sure what the attitude of a new acquaintance will be, whether it will be rejective or accepting, until the contact has been made. This is exactly the posi-

---

[24] From *Clinical Studies in Psychiatry*, H. S. Perry, M. L. Gawel, and M. Gibbon, eds. (New York: W. W. Norton & Company, 1956), p. 145.

[25] R. Barker, "The Social Psychology of Physical Disability," *Journal of Social Issues*, IV (1948), 34, suggests that stigmatized persons "live on a social-psychological frontier," constantly facing new situations. See also Macgregor *et al.*, *op. cit.*, p. 87, where the suggestion is made that the grossly deformed need suffer less doubt about their reception in interaction than the less visibly deformed.

tion of the adolescent, the light-skinned Negro, the second generation immigrant, the socially mobile person and the woman who has entered a predominantly masculine occupation.[26]

This uncertainty arises not merely from the stigmatized individual's not knowing which of several categories he will be placed in, but also, where the placement is favorable, from his knowing that in their hearts the others may be defining him in terms of his stigma:

> And I always feel this with straight people—that whenever they're being nice to me, pleasant to me, all the time really, underneath they're only assessing me as a criminal and nothing else. It's too late for me to be any different now to what I am, but I still feel this keenly, that that's their only approach, and they're quite incapable of accepting me as anything else.[27]

Thus in the stigmatized arises the sense of not knowing what the others present are "really" thinking about him.

Further, during mixed contacts, the stigmatized individual is likely to feel that he is "on,"[28] having to be self-conscious and calculating about the impression he is making, to a degree and in areas of conduct which he assumes others are not.

Also, he is likely to feel that the usual scheme of interpretation for everyday events has been undermined. His minor accomplishments, he feels, may be assessed as signs of remarkable and noteworthy capacities in the circumstances. A professional criminal provides an illustration:

> "You know, it's really amazing you should read books like this, I'm staggered I am. I should've thought you'd read paper-backed thrillers, things with lurid covers, books like that. And here you are with Claud Cockburn, Hugh Klare, Simone de Beauvoir, and Lawrence Durrell!"

[26] Barker, *op. cit.*, p. 33.
[27] Parker and Allerton, *op. cit.*, p. 111.
[28] This special kind of self-consciousness is analyzed in S. Messinger *et al.*, "Life as Theater: Some Notes on the Dramaturgic Approach to Social Reality," *Sociometry*, XXV (1962), 98-110.

STIGMA AND SOCIAL IDENTITY 15

> You know, he didn't see this as an insulting remark at all: in fact, I think he thought he was being honest in telling me how mistaken he was. And that's exactly the sort of patronizing you get from straight people if you're a criminal. "Fancy that!" they say. "In some ways you're just like a human being!" I'm not kidding, it makes me want to choke the bleeding life out of them.[29]

A blind person provides another illustration:

> His once most ordinary deeds—walking nonchalantly up the street, locating the peas on his plate, lighting a cigarette—are no longer ordinary. He becomes an unusual person. If he performs them with finesse and assurance they excite the same kind of wonderment inspired by a magician who pulls rabbits out of hats.[30]

At the same time, minor failings or incidental impropriety may, he feels, be interpreted as a direct expression of his stigmatized differentness. Ex-mental patients, for example, are sometimes afraid to engage in sharp interchanges with spouse or employer because of what a show of emotion might be taken as a sign of. Mental defectives face a similar contingency:

> It also happens that if a person of low intellectual ability gets into some sort of trouble the difficulty is more or less automatically attributed to "mental defect" whereas if a person of "normal intelligence" gets into a similar difficulty, it is not regarded as symptomatic of anything in particular.[31]

A one-legged girl, recalling her experience with sports, provides other illustrations:

> Whenever I fell, out swarmed the women in droves, clucking and fretting like a bunch of bereft mother hens. It was kind of them, and

---
[29] Parker and Allerton, *op. cit.*, p. 111.
[30] Chevigny, *op. cit.*, p. 140.
[31] L. A. Dexter, "A Social Theory of Mental Deficiency," *American Journal of Mental Deficiency*, LXII (1958), 923. For another study of the mental defective as a stigmatized person, see S. E. Perry, "Some Theoretical Problems of Mental Deficiency and Their Action Implications," *Psychiatry*, XVII (1954), 45-73.

in retrospect I appreciate their solicitude, but at the time I resented and was greatly embarrassed by their interference. For they assumed that no routine hazard to skating—no stick or stone—upset my flying wheels. It was a foregone conclusion that *I* fell because I was a poor, helpless cripple.[32]

Not one of them shouted with outrage, "That dangerous wild bronco threw her!"—which, God forgive, he did technically. It was like a horrible ghostly visitation of my old roller-skating days. All the good people lamented in chorus, "That poor, poor girl fell off!"[33]

When the stigmatized person's failing can be perceived by our merely directing attention (typically, visual) to him—when, in short, he is a discredited, not discreditable, person—he is likely to feel that to be present among normals nakedly exposes him to invasions of privacy,[34] experienced most pointedly perhaps when children simply stare at him.[35] This displeasure in being exposed can be increased by the conversations strangers may feel free to strike up with him, conversations in which they express what he takes to be morbid curiosity about his condition, or in which they proffer help that he does not need or want.[36] One might add that there are certain classic formulae for these kinds of conversations: "My dear girl, how did you get your quiggle"; "My great uncle had a quiggle, so I feel I know all about your problem"; "You know I've always said that Quiggles are good family men and look after their own poor"; "Tell me, how do you manage to bathe with a quiggle?" The implication of these overtures is that the stigmatized individual is a person who can be approached by strangers at will, providing only that they are sympathetic to the plight of persons of his kind.

[32] Baker, *Out on a Limb* (New York: McGraw-Hill Book Company, n.d.), p. 22.
[33] *Ibid.*, p. 73.
[34] This theme is well treated in R. K. White, B. A. Wright, and T. Dembo, "Studies in Adjustment to Visible Injuries: Evaluation of Curiosity by the Injured," *Journal of Abnormal and Social Psychology*, XLIII (1948), 13-28.
[35] For example, Henrich and Kriegel, *op. cit.*, p. 184.
[36] See Wright, *op. cit.*, "The Problem of Sympathy," pp. 233-237

Given what the stigmatized individual may well face upon entering a mixed social situation, he may anticipatorily respond by defensive cowering. This may be illustrated from an early study of some German unemployed during the Depression, the words being those of a 43-year-old mason:

> How hard and humiliating it is to bear the name of an unemployed man. When I go out, I cast down my eyes because I feel myself wholly inferior. When I go along the street, it seems to me that I can't be compared with an average citizen, that everybody is pointing at me with his finger. I instinctively avoid meeting anyone. Former acquaintances and friends of better times are no longer so cordial. They greet me indifferently when we meet. They no longer offer me a cigarette and their eyes seem to say, "You are not worth it, you don't work." [37]

A crippled girl provides an illustrative analysis:

> When . . . I began to walk out alone in the streets of our town . . . I found then that wherever I had to pass three or four children together on the sidewalk, if I happened to be alone, they would shout at me, . . . Sometimes they even ran after me, shouting and jeering. This was something I didn't know how to face, and it seemed as if I couldn't bear it. . . .
>
> For awhile those encounters in the street filled me with a cold dread of all unknown children . . .
>
> One day I suddenly realized that I had become so self-conscious and afraid of all strange children that, like animals, they knew I was afraid, so that even the mildest and most amiable of them were automatically prompted to derision by my own shrinking and dread.[38]

Instead of cowering, the stigmatized individual may attempt to approach mixed contacts with hostile bravado, but this can

---

[37] S. Zawadski and P. Lazarsfeld, "The Psychological Consequences of Unemployment," *Journal of Social Psychology*, VI (1935), 239.

[38] Hathaway, *op. cit.*, pp. 155-157, in S. Richardson, "The Social Psychological Consequences of Handicapping," unpublished paper presented at the 1962 American Sociological Association Convention, Washington, D. C., 7-8.

induce from others its own set of troublesome reciprocations. It may be added that the stigmatized person sometimes vacillates between cowering and bravado, racing from one to the other, thus demonstrating one central way in which ordinary face-to-face interaction can run wild.

I am suggesting, then, that the stigmatized individual—at least the "visibly" stigmatized one—will have special reasons for feeling that mixed social situations make for anxious unanchored interaction. But if this is so, then it is to be suspected that we normals will find these situations shaky too. We will feel that the stigmatized individual is either too aggressive or too shamefaced, and in either case too ready to read unintended meanings into our actions. We ourselves may feel that if we show direct sympathetic concern for his condition, we may be overstepping ourselves; and yet if we actually forget that he has a failing we are likely to make impossible demands of him or unthinkingly slight his fellow-sufferers. Each potential source of discomfort for him when we are with him can become something we sense he is aware of, aware that we are aware of, and even aware of our state of awareness about his awareness; the stage is then set for the infinite regress of mutual consideration that Meadian social psychology tells us how to begin but not how to terminate.

Given what both the stigmatized and we normals introduce into mixed social situations, it is understandable that all will not go smoothly. We are likely to attempt to carry on as though in fact he wholly fitted one of the types of person naturally available to us in the situation, whether this means treating him as someone better than we feel he might be or someone worse than we feel he probably is. If neither of these tacks is possible, then we may try to act as if he were a "non-person," and not present at all as someone of whom ritual notice is to be taken. He, in turn, is likely to go along with these strategies, at least initially.

In consequence, attention is furtively withdrawn from its obligatory targets, and self-consciousness and "other-consciousness" occurs, expressed in the pathology of interaction—uneasiness.[39] As described in the case of the physically handicapped:

> Whether the handicap is overtly and tactlessly responded to as such or, as is more commonly the case, no explicit reference is made to it, the underlying condition of heightened, narrowed, awareness causes the interaction to be articulated too exclusively in terms of it. This, as my informants described it, is usually accompanied by one or more of the familiar signs of discomfort and stickiness: the guarded references, the common everyday words suddenly made taboo, the fixed stare elsewhere, the artificial levity, the compulsive loquaciousness, the awkward solemnity.[40]

In social situations with an individual known or perceived to have a stigma, we are likely, then, to employ categorizations that do not fit, and we and he are likely to experience uneasiness. Of course, there is often significant movement from this starting point. And since the stigmatized person is likely to be more often faced with these situations than are we, he is likely to become the more adept at managing them.

The Own and the Wise

Earlier it was suggested that a discrepancy may exist between an individual's virtual and actual identity. This discrepancy, when known about or apparent, spoils his social identity; it has the effect of cutting him off from society and from himself so that he stands a discredited person facing an unaccepting world. In some cases, as with the individual who is born without a nose, he may continue through life to find that he is the only one of his kind and that all the world is against him. In most cases, however, he will find that there are sympathetic others who are ready to adopt his standpoint in the world and to share with him

---

[39] For a general treatment, see E. Goffman, "Alienation from Interaction," *Human Relations*, X (1957), 47-60.
[40] F. Davis, "Deviance Disavowal: The Management of Strained Interaction by the Visibly Handicapped," *Social Problems*, IX (1961), 123. See also White, Wright, and Dembo, *op. cit.*, pp. 26-27.

the feeling that he is human and "essentially" normal in spite of appearances and in spite of his own self-doubts. Two such categories will be considered.

The first set of sympathetic others is of course those who share his stigma. Knowing from their own experience what it is like to have this particular stigma, some of them can provide the individual with instruction in the tricks of the trade and with a circle of lament to which he can withdraw for moral support and for the comfort of feeling at home, at ease, accepted as a person who really is like any other normal person. One example may be cited from a study of illiterates:

> The existence of a different value system among these persons is evinced by the communality of behavior which occurs when illiterates interact among themselves. Not only do they change from unexpressive and confused individuals, as they frequently appear in larger society, to expressive and understanding persons within their own group, but moreover they express themselves in institutional terms. Among themselves they have a universe of response. They form and recognize symbols of prestige and disgrace; evaluate relevant situations in terms of their own norms and in their own idiom: and in their interrelations with one another, the mask of accommodative adjustment drops.[41]

Another from the hard of hearing:

> I remembered how relaxing it was, at Nitchie School, to be with people who took impaired hearing for granted. Now I wanted to know some people who took hearing aids for granted. How restful it would be to adjust the volume control on my transmitter without caring whether or not anyone was looking. To stop thinking, for awhile, about whether the cord at the back of my neck was showing. What luxury to say out loud to someone, "Ye gods, my battery's dead!"[42]

[41] H. Freeman and G. Kasenbaum, "The Illiterate in America," *Social Forces,* XXXIV (1956), 374.
[42] Warfield, *op. cit.*, p. 60.

Among his own, the stigmatized individual can use his disadvantage as a basis for organizing life, but he must resign himself to a half-world to do so. Here he may develop to its fullest his sad tale accounting for his possession of the stigma. The explanations produced by the mentally defective to account for admission to the institution for their kind provide an example:

> (1) "I got mixed up with a gang. One night we were robbing a gas station and the cops got me. I don't belong here." (2) "You know, I shouldn't be here at all. I'm epileptic, I don't belong here with these other people." (3) "My parents hate me and put me in here." (4) "They say I'm crazy. I'm not crazy, but even if I was, I don't belong in here with these low-grades." [43]

On the other hand, he may find that the tales of his fellow-sufferers bore him, and that the whole matter of focusing on atrocity tales, on group superiority, on trickster stories, in short, on the "problem," is one of the large penalties for having one. Behind this focus on the problem is, of course, a perspective not so much different from that of the normal as it is specialized in one sector:

> We all seem to be inclined to identify people with characteristics which are of importance to us, or which we think must be of general importance. If you asked a person who the late Franklin D. Roosevelt was, he would probably answer that Roosevelt was the 32nd president of the United States, not that he was a man suffering from polio, although many persons, of course, would have mentioned his polio as supplementary information, considering it an interesting fact that he managed to fight his way to the White House in spite of this handicap. The cripple, however, would probably think of Mr. Roosevelt's polio when he heard his name mentioned.[44]

[43] R. Edgerton and G. Sabagh, "From Mortification to Aggrandizement: Changing Self-Concepts in the Careers of the Mentally Retarded," *Psychiatry*, XXV (1962), 268. For further comment on sad tales, see E. Goffman, "The Moral Career of the Mental Patient," *Psychiatry*, XXII (1959), 133-134.

[44] Carling, *op. cit.*, pp. 18-19.

In the sociological study of stigmatized persons, one is usually concerned with the kind of corporate life, if any, that is sustained by those of a particular category. Certainly here one finds a fairly full catalogue of types of group formation and types of group function. There are speech defectives whose peculiarity apparently discourages any group formation whatsoever.[45] On the boundaries of a willingness to unite are ex-mental patients— only a relatively small number are currently willing to support mental health clubs, in spite of innocuous club titles which allow members to come together under a plain wrapper.[46] Then there are the huddle-together self-help clubs formed by the divorced, the aged, the obese, the physically handicapped,[47] the ileostomied and colostomied.[48] There are residential clubs, voluntary to varying degrees, formed for the ex-alcoholic and the ex-addict. There are national associations such as AA which provide a full doctrine and almost a way of life for their members. Often these associations are the culmination of years of effort on the part of variously situated persons and groups, providing exemplary objects of study as social movements.[49] There are mutual-claims networks formed by ex-convicts from the same prison or reformatory, an example of which is the tacit society claimed to

[45] E. Lemert, *Social Pathology* (New York: McGraw-Hill Book Company, 1951), p. 151.
[46] A general survey is provided in H. Wechsler, "The Expatient Organization: A Survey," *Journal of Social Issues*, XVI (1960), 47-53. Titles include: Recovery, Inc., Search, Club 103, Fountain House Foundation, San Francisco Fellowship Club, Center Club. For a study of one such club, see D. Landy and S. Singer, "The Social Organization and Culture of a Club for Former Mental Patients," *Human Relations*, XIV (1961), 31-41. See also M. B. Palmer, "Social Rehabilitation for Mental Patients," *Mental Hygiene*, XLII (1958), 24-28.
[47] See Baker, *op. cit.*, pp. 158-159.
[48] D. R. White, "I have an ileostomy . . . I wish I didn't. But I have learned to Accept it and Live a Normal, Full Life," *American Journal of Nursing*, LXI (1961), 52: "At this time, ileostomy and colostomy clubs exist in 16 states and the District of Columbia as well as in Australia, Canada, England, and South Africa."
[49] Warfield, *op. cit.*, pp. 135-136, describes a 1950 celebration of the New York hard of hearing movement, with every successive generation of leadership present, as well as representatives of every originally separate organization. A complete recapitulation of the movement's history was thus available. For comments on the international history of the movement, see K. W. Hodgson, *The Deaf and their Problems* (New York: Philosophical Library, 1954), p. 352.

exist in South America of escapees from the French penal settlement in French Guiana;[50] more traditionally, there are national networks of acquainted individuals (or acquainted once-removed) to which some criminals and some homosexuals seem to belong. There are also urban milieux containing a nucleus of service institutions which provide a territorial base for prostitutes, drug addicts, homosexuals, alcoholics, and other shamed groups, these establishments being sometimes shared by outcasts of different kinds, sometimes not. Finally, within the city, there are full-fledged residential communities, ethnic, racial, or religious, with a high concentration of tribally stigmatized persons and (in contradistinction to much other group formation among the stigmatized) the family, not the individual, as the basic unit of organization.

Here, of course, there is a common conceptual confusion. The term "category" is perfectly abstract and can be applied to any aggregate, in this case persons with a particular stigma. A good portion of those who fall within a given stigma category may well refer to the total membership by the term "group" or an equivalent, such as "we," or "our people." Those outside the category may similarly designate those within it in group terms. However, often in such cases the full membership will not be part of a single group, in the strictest sense; they will neither have a capacity for collective action, nor a stable and embracing pattern of mutual interaction. What one does find is that the members of a particular stigma category will have a tendency to come together into small social groups whose members all derive from the category, these groups themselves being subject to overarching organization to varying degrees. And one also finds that when one member of the category happens to come into contact with another, both may be disposed to modify their treatment of each other by virtue of believing that they each belong to the same "group." Further, in being a member of the category, an individual may have an increased probability of coming into contact with any other member, and even forming a relation-

[50] Reported in F. Poli, *Gentlemen Convicts* (London: Rupert Hart-Davis, 1960).

ship with him as a result. A category, then, can function to dispose its members to group-formation and relationships, but its total membership does not thereby constitute a group—a conceptual nicety that will hereafter not always be observed in this essay.

Whether or not those with a particular stigma provide the recruitment base for a community that is ecologically consolidated in some way, they are likely to support agents and agencies who represent them. (Interestingly, we have no word to designate accurately the constituents, following, fans, subjects, or supporters of such representatives.) Members may, for example, have an office or lobby to push their case with the Press or Government, differing here in terms of whether they can have a man of their own kind, a "native" who really knows, as do the deaf, the blind, the alcoholic, and Jews, or someone from the other side, as do ex-cons and the mentally defective.[51] (Action groups which serve the same category of stigmatized person may sometimes be in slight opposition to each other, and this opposition will often reflect a difference between management by natives and management by normals.) A characteristic task of these representatives is to convince the public to use a softer social label for the category in question:

> Acting on this conviction, the League [New York League for the Hard of Hearing] staff agreed to use only such terms as hard of hearing, impaired hearing, and hearing loss; to excise the word deaf from their conversation, their correspondence and other writings, their teaching, and their speeches in public. It worked. New York in general gradually began to use the new vocabulary. Straight thinking was on the way.[52]

Another of their usual tasks is to appear as "speakers" before various audiences of normals and of the stigmatized; they present the case for the stigmatized and, when they themselves are

---

[51] For example, see Chevigny, *op. cit.*, Chap. 5, where the situation is presented regarding the blind.
[52] Warfield, *op. cit.*, p. 78.

natives of the group, provide a living model of fully-normal achievement, being heroes of adjustment who are subject to public awards for proving that an individual of this kind can be a good person.

Often those with a particular stigma sponsor a publication of some kind which gives voice to shared feelings, consolidating and stabilizing for the reader his sense of the realness of "his" group and his attachment to it. Here the ideology of the members is formulated—their complaints, their aspirations, their politics. The names of well-known friends and enemies of the "group" are cited, along with information to confirm the goodness or the badness of these people. Success stories are printed, tales of heroes of assimilation who have penetrated new areas of normal acceptance. Atrocity tales are recorded, recent and historic, of extreme mistreatment by normals. Exemplary moral tales are provided in biographical and autobiographical form illustrating a desirable code of conduct for the stigmatized. The publication also serves as a forum for presenting some division of opinion as to how the situation of the stigmatized person ought best to be handled. Should the individual's failing require special equipment, it is here advertised and reviewed. The readership of these publications provides a market for books and pamphlets which present a similar line.

It is important to stress that, in America at least, no matter how small and how badly off a particular stigmatized category is, the viewpoint of its members is likely to be given public presentation of some kind. It can thus be said that Americans who are stigmatized tend to live in a literarily-defined world, however uncultured they might be. If they don't read books on the situation of persons like themselves, they at least read magazines and see movies; and where they don't do these, then they listen to local, vocal associates. An intellectually worked-up version of their point of view is thus available to most stigmatized persons.

A comment is here required about those who come to serve as representatives of a stigmatized category. Starting out as someone who is a little more vocal, a little better known, or a little better connected than his fellow-sufferers, a stigmatized person may find that the "movement" has absorbed his whole day, and that he has become a professional. This end point is illustrated by a hard of hearing:

> In 1942 I was spending almost every day at the League. Mondays I sewed with the Red Cross Unit. Tuesdays I worked in the office, typing and filing, operating the switchboard in a pinch. Wednesday afternoons I assisted the doctor at the League's deafness-prevention clinic at Manhattan Eye and Ear Hospital, a job I particularly enjoyed—keeping records on children who, because their head colds, running ears, infections, and potentially deafening after-effects of childhood diseases were getting the benefit of new knowledge, new drugs, and new otological techniques, probably would not be growing up with cotton in their ears. Thursday afternoons I sat in on League adult lip-reading classes and afterwards we all played cards and drank tea. Fridays I worked on the *Bulletin*. Saturdays I made egg-salad sandwiches and cocoa. Once a month I attended the meeting of the Women's Auxiliary, a volunteer group organized in 1921 by Mrs. Wendell Phillips and other interested otologists' wives to raise funds, promote membership, and represent the League socially. I made Halloween favors for the six-year-olds and helped serve the Old Timers' Thanksgiving Dinner. I wrote the Christmas mail appeal for contributions, helped address the envelopes and lick the the stamps. I hung the new curtains and mended the old ping-pong table; chaperoned the young people's Valentine Dance and manned a booth at the Easter Bazaar.[53]

It might be added that once a person with a particular stigma attains high occupational, political, or financial position—how high depending on the stigmatized group in question—a new career is likely to be thrust upon him, that of representing his category. He finds himself too eminent to avoid being presented by his own as an instance of them. (The weakness of a stigma

[53] Warfield, *op. cit.*, pp. 73-74; see also Chap. 9, pp. 129-158, where a kind of confession is provided regarding the professional life. For a description of life as a professional amputee, see H. Russell, *Victory in My Hands* (New York: Creative Age Press, 1949).

can thus be measured by how eminent a member of the category may be and yet manage to avoid these pressures.)

Two points are sometimes made about this kind of professionalization. First, in making a profession of their stigma, native leaders are obliged to have dealings with representatives of other categories, and so find themselves breaking out of the closed circle of their own kind. Instead of leaning on their crutch, they get to play golf with it, ceasing, in terms of social participation, to be representative of the people they represent.[54]

Secondly, those who professionally present the viewpoint of their category may introduce some systematic bias in this presentation simply because they are sufficiently involved in the problem to write about it. Although any particular stigma category is likely to have professionals who take different lines, and may even support publications which advocate different programs, there is uniform tacit agreement that the situation of the individual with this particular stigma is worth attention. Whether a writer takes a stigma very seriously or makes light of it, he must define it as something worth writing about. This minimal agreement, even when there are no others, helps to consolidate belief in the stigma as a basis for self-conception. Here again representatives are not representative, for representation can hardly come from those who give no attention to their stigma, or who are relatively unlettered.

I do not mean to suggest here that professionals provide the stigmatized with the sole public source of reminder as to their situation in life; there are other reminders. Each time someone with a particular stigma makes a spectacle of himself by breaking a law, winning a prize, or becoming a first of his kind, a local community may take gossipy note of this; these events can even make news in the mass media of the wider society. In any case, they who share the noted person's stigma suddenly become accessible to the normals immediately around and become subject

[54] From the beginning such leaders may be recruited from those members of the category who are ambitious to leave the life of its members and relatively able to do so, giving rise to what Lewin (*op. cit.*, pp. 195-196) called "Leadership from the Periphery."

to a slight transfer of credit or discredit to themselves. Their situation thus leads them easily into living in a world of publicized heroes and villains of their own stripe, their relation to this world being underlined by immediate associates, both normal and otherwise, who bring them news about how one of their kind has fared.

I have considered one set of individuals from whom the stigmatized person can expect some support: those who share his stigma and by virtue of this are defined and define themselves as his own kind. The second set are—to borrow a term once used by homosexuals—the "wise," namely, persons who are normal but whose special situation has made them intimately privy to the secret life of the stigmatized individual and sympathetic with it, and who find themselves accorded a measure of acceptance, a measure of courtesy membership in the clan. Wise persons are the marginal men before whom the individual with a fault need feel no shame nor exert self-control, knowing that in spite of his failing he will be seen as an ordinary other. An example may be cited from the world of prostitutes:

> Although she sneers at respectability, the prostitute, particularly the call girl, is supersensitive in polite society, taking refuge in her off hours with Bohemian artists, writers, actors and would-be intellectuals. There she may be accepted as an off-beat personality, without being a curiosity.[55]

Before taking the standpoint of those with a particular stigma, the normal person who is becoming wise may first have to pass through a heart-changing personal experience, of which there are many literary records.[56] And after the sympathetic normal makes himself available to the stigmatized, he often must wait their validation of him as a courtesy member. The self must not

[55] J. Stearn, *Sisters of the Night* (New York: Popular Library, 1961), p. 181.
[56] N. Mailer, "The Homosexual Villain," in *Advertisements for Myself* (New York: Signet Books, 1960), pp. 200-205, provides a model confession detailing the basic cycle of bigotry, enlightening experience, and, finally, recantation of prejudice through public admission. See also Angus Wilson's introduction to Carling, *op. cit.*, for a confessional record of Wilson's redefinition of cripples.

STIGMA AND SOCIAL IDENTITY

only be offered, it must be accepted. Sometimes, of course, the final step does seem to be initiated by the normal; the following is an example of this

> I don't know whether I can or not, but let me tell of an incident. I was once admitted to a group of Negro boys of about my own age with whom I used to fish. When I first began to join them, they would carefully use the term "Negro" in my presence. Gradually, as we went fishing more and more often, they began to joke with each other in front of me and to call each other "nigger." The real change was in their utilization of the word "nigger" when joking after the previous inability to use the word "nigger" at all.
> One day when we were swimming, a boy shoved me with mock violence and I said to him, "Don't give me that nigger talk."
> He replied, "You bastard," with a big grin.
> From that time on, we could all use the word "nigger" but the old categories had totally changed. Never, as long as I live, will I forget the way my stomach felt after I used the word "nigger" without any reservation.[57]

One type of wise person is he whose wiseness comes from working in an establishment which caters either to the wants of those with a particular stigma or to actions that society takes in regard to these persons. For example, nurses and physical therapists can be wise; they can come to know more about a given type of prosthetic equipment than the patient who must learn to use it so as to minimize his disfigurement. Gentile employees in delicatessens are often wise, as are straight bartenders in homosexual bars, and the maids of Mayfair prostitutes.[58] The police, in constantly having to deal with criminals, may become wise in regard to them, leading a professional to suggest that ". . . in fact the police are the only people apart from other criminals who accept you for what you are."[59]

[57] Ray Birdwhistell in B. Schaffner, ed., *Group Processes*, Transactions of the Second (1955) Conference (New York: Josiah Macy, Jr. Foundation, 1956), p. 171.
[58] C. H. Rolph, ed., *Women of the Streets* (London: Secker and Warburg, 1955), pp. 78-79.
[59] Parker and Allerton, *op. cit.*, p. 150.

A second type of wise person is the individual who is related through the social structure to a stigmatized individual—a relationship that leads the wider society to treat both individuals in some respects as one. Thus the loyal spouse of the mental patient, the daughter of the ex-con, the parent of the cripple, the friend of the blind, the family of the hangman,[60] are all obliged to share some of the discredit of the stigmatized person to whom they are related. One response to this fate is to embrace it, and to live within the world of one's stigmatized connection. It should be added that persons who acquire a degree of stigma in this way can themselves have connections who acquire a little of the disease twice-removed. The problems faced by stigmatized persons spread out in waves, but of diminishing intensity. A newspaper advice column provides an illustration:

Dear Ann Landers:

I'm a girl 12 years old who is left out of all social activities because my father is an ex-convict. I try to be nice and friendly to everyone but it's no use. The girls at school have told me that their mothers don't want them to associate with me because it will be bad for their reputations. My father had some bad publicity in the papers and even though he has served his time nobody will forget it.

Is there anything I can do? I am very lonesome because it's no fun to be alone all the time. My mother tries to take me places with her but I want to be with people my own age. Please give me some advice—An OUTCAST.[61]

In general, the tendency for a stigma to spread from the stigmatized individual to his close connections provides a reason why such relations tend either to be avoided or to be terminated, where existing.

Persons with a courtesy stigma provide a model of "normalization," [62] showing how far normals could go in treating the stig-

[60] J. Atholl, *The Reluctant Hangman* (London: John Long, Ltd., 1956), p. 61.
[61] *Berkeley Daily Gazette*, April 12, 1961.
[62] The idea derives from C. G. Schwartz, "Perspectives on Deviance—Wives' Definitions of Their Husbands' Mental Illness," *Psychiatry*, XX (1957), 275-291.

matized person as if he didn't have a stigma. (Normalization is to be distinguished from "normification," namely, the effort on the part of a stigmatized individual to present himself as an ordinary person, although not necessarily making a secret of his failing.) Further, a cult of the stigmatized can occur, the stigmaphobic response of the normal being countered by the stigmaphile response of the wise. The person with a courtesy stigma can in fact make both the stigmatized and the normal uncomfortable: by always being ready to carry a burden that is not "really" theirs, they can confront everyone else with too much morality; by treating the stigma as a neutral matter to be looked at in a direct, off-hand way, they open themselves and the stigmatized to misunderstanding by normals who may read offensiveness into this behavior.[63]

The relation between the stigmatized and his stand-in can be an uneasy one. The person with a failing may feel that reversion to type may occur at any moment, and at a time when defenses are down and dependency is up. Thus a prostitute:

> Well, I want to see what I can do with acting first. I've explained to him that if we were married and had a fight, he'd throw it up to me. He said no, but that's the way men are.[64]

On the other hand, the individual with a courtesy stigma may find that he must suffer many of the standard deprivations of his courtesy group and yet not be able to enjoy the self-elevation which is a common defense against such treatment. Further, much like the stigmatized in regard to him, he can doubt that in the last analysis he is really "accepted" by his courtesy group.[65]

---

[63] For an example in regard to the blind, see A. Gowman, "Blindness and the Role of the Companion," *Social Problems*, IV (1956), 68-75.
[64] Stearn, *op. cit.*, p. 99.
[65] The range of possibilities is nicely explored in C. Brossard, "Plaint of a Gentile Intellectual," in Brossard, ed., *The Scene Before You* (New York: Holt, Rinehart & Winston, 1955), pp. 87-91.

Moral Career

Persons who have a particular stigma tend to have similar learning experiences regarding their plight, and similar changes in conception of self—a similar "moral career" that is both cause and effect of commitment to a similar sequence of personal adjustments. (The natural history of a category of persons with a stigma must be clearly distinguished from the natural history of the stigma itself—the history of the origins, spread, and decline of the capacity of an attribute to serve as a stigma in a particular society, for example, divorce in American upper middle class society.) One phase of this socialization process is that through which the stigmatized person learns and incorporates the standpoint of the normal, acquiring thereby the identity beliefs of the wider society and a general idea of what it would be like to possess a particular stigma. Another phase is that through which he learns that he possesses a particular stigma and, this time in detail, the consequence of possessing it. The timing and interplay of these two initial phases of the moral career form important patterns, establishing the foundation for later development, and providing a means of distinguishing among the moral careers available to the stigmatized. Four such patterns may be mentioned.

One pattern involves those with an inborn stigma who become socialized into their disadvantageous situation even while they are learning and incorporating the standards against which they fall short.[66] For example, an orphan learns that children naturally and normally have parents, even while he is learning what it means not to have any. After spending the first sixteen years of his life in the institution he can later still feel that he naturally knows how to be a father to his son.

A second pattern derives from the capacity of a family, and to a much lesser extent a local neighborhood, to constitute itself a protective capsule for its young. Within such a capsule a con-

[66] Discussion of this pattern can be found in A. R. Lindesmith and A. L. Strauss, *Social Psychology*, rev. ed. (New York: Holt, Rinehart & Winston, 1956), pp. 180-183.

genitally stigmatized child can be carefully sustained by means of information control. Self-belittling definitions of him are prevented from entering the charmed circle, while broad access is given to other conceptions held in the wider society, ones that lead the encapsulated child to see himself as a fully qualified ordinary human being, of normal identity in terms of such basic matters as age and sex.

The point in the protected individual's life when the domestic circle can no longer protect him will vary by social class, place of residence, and type of stigma, but in each case will give rise to a moral experience when it occurs. Thus, public school entrance is often reported as the occasion of stigma learning, the experience sometimes coming very precipitously on the first day of school, with taunts, teasing, ostracism, and fights.[67] Interestingly, the more the child is "handicapped" the more likely he is to be sent to a special school for persons of his kind, and the more abruptly he will have to face the view which the public at large takes of him. He will be told that he will have an easier time of it among "his own," and thus learn that the own he thought he possessed was the wrong one, and that this lesser own is really his. It should be added that where the infantilely stigmatized manages to get through his early school years with some illusions left, the onset of dating or job-getting will often introduce the moment of truth. In some cases, merely an increased likelihood of incidental disclosure is involved:

> I think the first realization of my situation, and the first intense grief resulting from this realization, came one day, very casually, when a group of us in our early teens had gone to the beach for the day. I was lying on the sand, and I guess the fellows and girls thought I was asleep. One of the fellows said, "I like Domenica very much, but I would never go out with a blind girl." I cannot think of any prejudice which so completely rejects you.[68]

---

[67] An example from the experience of a blind person may be found in R. Criddle, *Love Is Not Blind* (New York: W. W. Norton & Company, 1953), p. 21; the experience of a dwarfed person is reported in H. Viscardi, Jr., *A Man's Stature* (New York: The John Day Company, 1952), pp. 13-14.

[68] Henrich and Kriegel, *op. cit.*, p. 186.

In other cases, something closer to systematic exposure is involved, as a cerebral palsy victim suggests:

> With one extremely painful exception, as long as I was in the protective custody of family life or college schedules and lived without exercising my rights as an adult citizen, the forces of society were kindly and unruffling. It was after college, business school, and innumerable stretches as a volunteer worker on community projects that I was often bogged down by the medieval prejudices and superstitions of the business world. Looking for a job was like standing before a firing squad. Employers were shocked that I had the gall to apply for a job.[69]

A third pattern of socialization is illustrated by one who becomes stigmatized late in life, or learns late in life that he has always been discreditable—the first involving no radical reorganization of his view of his past, the second involving this factor. Such an individual has thoroughly learned about the normal and the stigmatized long before he must see himself as deficient. Presumably he will have a special problem in re-identifying himself, and a special likelihood of developing disapproval of self:

> When I smelled an odor on the bus or subway before the colostomy I used to feel very annoyed. I'd think that the people were awful, that they didn't take a bath or that they should have gone to the bathroom before traveling. I used to think that they might have odors from what they ate. I used to be terribly annoyed; to me it seemed that they were filthy, dirty. Of course, at the least opportunity I used to change my seat and if I couldn't it used to go against my grain. So naturally, I believe that the young people feel the same way about me if I smell.[70]

While there are certainly cases of individuals discovering only in adult life that they belong to a stigmatized tribal group or

[69] *Ibid.*, p. 156.
[70] Orbach *et al.*, *op. cit.*, p. 165.

that their parents have a contagious moral blemish, the usual case here is that of physical handicaps that "strike" late in life:

> But suddenly I woke up one morning, and found that I could not stand. I had had polio, and polio was as simple as that. I was like a very young child who had been dropped into a big, black hole, and the only thing I was certain of was that I could not get out unless someone helped me. The education, the lectures, and the parental training which I had received for twenty-four years didn't seem to make me the person who could do anything for me now. I was like everyone else—normal, quarrelsome, gay, full of plans, and all of a sudden something happened! Something happened and I became a stranger. I was a greater stranger to myself than to anyone. Even my dreams did not know me. They did not know what they ought to let me do—and when I went to dances or to parties in them, there was always an odd provision or limitation—not spoken of or mentioned, but there just the same. I suddenly had the very confusing mental and emotional conflict of a lady leading a double life. It was unreal and it puzzled me, and I could not help dwelling on it.[71]

Here the medical profession is likely to have the special job of informing the infirm who he is going to have to be.

A fourth pattern is illustrated by those who are initially socialized in an alien community, whether inside or outside the geographical boundaries of the normal society, and who then must learn a second way of being that is felt by those around them to be the real and valid one.

It should be added that when an individual acquires a new stigmatized self late in life, the uneasiness he feels about new associates may slowly give way to uneasiness felt concerning old ones. Post-stigma acquaintances may see him simply as a faulted person; pre-stigma acquaintances, being attached to a conception of what he once was, may be unable to treat him either with formal tact or with familiar full acceptance:

> My task [as a blind writer interviewing prospective clients for his literary product] was to put the men I'd come to see at their ease—

[71] N. Linduska, *My Polio Past* (Chicago: Pellegrini and Cudahy, 1947), p. 177.

the reverse of the usual situation. Curiously, I found it much easier to do with men I'd never met before. Perhaps this was because with strangers there was no body of reminiscences to cover before business could be gotten down to and so there was no unpleasant contrast with the present.[72]

Regardless of which general pattern the moral career of the stigmatized individual illustrates, the phase of experience during which he learns that he possesses a stigma will be especially interesting, for at this time he is likely to be thrown into a new relationship to others who possess the stigma too.

In some cases, the only contact the individual will have with his own is a fleeting one, but sufficient nonetheless to show him that others like himself exist:

> When Tommy came to the clinic the first time, there were two other little boys there, each with a congenital absence of an ear. When Tommy saw them, his right hand went slowly to his own defective ear, and he turned with wide eyes to his father and said, "There's another boy with an ear like mine." [73]

In the case of the individual who has recently become physically handicapped, fellow-sufferers more advanced than himself in dealing with the failing are likely to make him a special series of visits to welcome him to the club and to instruct him in how to manage himself physically and psychically:

> Almost my first awareness that there are mechanics of adjustment came to me with the comparison of two fellow patients I had at the Eye and Ear Infirmary. They used to visit me as I lay abed and I came to know them fairly well. Both had been blind for seven years. They were about the same age—a little past thirty—and both had college educations.[74]

In the many cases where the individual's stigmatization is associated with his admission to a custodial institution such as a

[72] Chevigny, *op. cit.*, p. 136.
[73] Macgregor *et al.*, *op. cit.*, pp. 19-20.
[74] Chevigny, *op. cit.*, p. 35.

jail, sanatorium, or orphanage, much of what he learns about his stigma will be transmitted to him during prolonged intimate contact with those in the process of being transformed into his fellow-sufferers.

As already suggested, when the individual first learns who it is that he must now accept as his own, he is likely, at the very least, to feel some ambivalence; for these others will not only be patently stigmatized, and thus not like the normal person he knows himself to be, but may also have other attributes with which he finds it difficult to associate himself. What may end up as a freemasonry may begin with a shudder. A newly blind girl on a visit to The Lighthouse directly from leaving the hospital provides an illustration:

> My questions about a guide dog were politely turned aside. Another sighted worker took me in tow to show me around. We visited the Braille library; the classrooms; the clubrooms where the blind members of the music and dramatic groups meet; the recreation hall where on festive occasion the blind dance with the blind; the bowling alleys where the blind play together; the cafeteria, where all the blind gather to eat together; the huge workshops where the blind earn a subsistence income by making mops and brooms, weaving rugs, caning chairs. As we moved from room to room, I could hear the shuffling of feet, the muted voices, the tap-tap-tapping of canes. Here was the safe, segregated world of the sightless—a completely different world, I was assured by the social worker, from the one I had just left. . . .
>
> I was expected to join this world. To give up my profession and to earn my living making mops. The Lighthouse would be happy to teach me how to make mops. I was to spend the rest of my life making mops with other blind people, eating with other blind people, dancing with other blind people. I became nauseated with fear, as the picture grew in my mind. Never had I come upon such destructive segregation.[75]

---

[75] Keitlen, *op. cit.*, pp. 37-38. A description of the early vicissitudes of a hospitalized polio patient's identification with fellow-cripples is provided in Linduska, *op. cit.*, pp. 159-165. A fictional account of racial re-identification is provided by J. W. Johnson, *The Autobiography of an Ex-Coloured Man*, rev. ed. (New York: Hill and Wang, American Century Series, 1960), pp. 22-23.

Given the ambivalence built into the individual's attachment to his stigmatized category, it is understandable that oscillations may occur in his support of, identification with, and participation among his own. There will be "affiliation cycles" through which he comes to accept the special opportunities for in-group participation or comes to reject them after having accepted them before.[76] There will be corresponding oscillations in belief about the nature of own group and the nature of normals. For example, adolescence (and the high school peer group) can bring a marked decline in own-group identification and a marked increase in identification with normals.[77] The later phases of the individual's moral career are to be found in these shifts of participation and belief.

The relationship of the stigmatized individual to the informal community and formal organizations of his own kind is, then, crucial. This relationship will, for example, mark a great difference between those whose differentness provides them very little of a new "we," and those, such as minority group members, who find themselves a part of a well-organized community with longstanding traditions—a community that makes appreciable claims on loyalty and income, defining the member as someone who should take pride in his illness and not seek to get well. In any case, whether the stigmatized group is an established one or not, it is largely in relation to this own-group that it is possible to discuss the natural history and the moral career of the stigmatized individual.

In reviewing his own moral career, the stigmatized individual may single out and retrospectively elaborate experiences which serve for him to account for his coming to the beliefs and practices that he now has regarding his own kind and normals. A life event can thus have a double bearing on moral career, first as immediate objective grounds for an actual turning point, and

---

[76] A general statement may be found in two of E. C. Hughes' papers, "Social Change and Status Protest," *Phylon*, First Quarter, 1949, 58-65, and "Cycles and Turning Points," in *Men and Their Work* (New York: Free Press of Glencoe, 1958).

[77] M. Yarrow, "Personality Development and Minority Group Membership," in M. Sklare, *The Jews* (New York: Free Press of Glencoe, 1960), pp. 468-470.

later (and easier to demonstrate) as a means of accounting for a position currently taken. One experience often selected for this latter purpose is that through which the newly stigmatized individual learns that full-fledged members of the group are quite like ordinary human beings:

> When I [a young girl turning to a life of vice and first meeting her madam] turned into Fourth Street my courage again failed me, and I was about to beat a retreat when Mamie came out of a restaurant across the street and warmly greeted me. The porter, who came to the door in response to our ring, said that Miss Laura was in her room, and we were shown in. I saw a woman comely and middle-aged, who bore no resemblance to the horrible creature of my imagination. She greeted me in a soft, well-bred voice, and everything about her so eloquently spoke of her potentialities for motherhood that instinctively I looked around for the children who should have been clinging to her skirts.[78]

Another illustration is provided by a homosexual in regard to his becoming one:

> I met a man with whom I had been at school. . . . He was, of course, gay himself, and took it for granted that I was, too. I was surprised and rather impressed. He did not look in the least like the popular idea of a homosexual, being well-built, masculine and neatly dressed. This was something new to me. Although I was perfectly prepared to admit that love could exist between men, I had always been slightly repelled by the obvious homosexuals whom I had met because of their vanity, their affected manner, and their ceaseless chatter. These, it now appeared, formed only a small part of the homosexual world, although the most noticeable one. . . .[79]

A cripple provides a similar statement:

> If I had to choose one group of experiences that finally convinced me of the importance of this problem [of self-image] and that I had

[78] *Madeleine, An Autobiography* (New York: Pyramid Books, 1961), pp. 36-37.
[79] P. Wildeblood, *Against the Law* (New York: Julian Messner, 1959), pp. 23-24.

to fight my own battles of identification, it would be the incidents that made me realize with my heart that cripples could be identified with characteristics other than their physical handicap. I managed to see that cripples could be comely, charming, ugly, lovely, stupid, brilliant—just like all other people, and I discovered that I was able to hate or love a cripple in spite of his handicap.[80]

It may be added that in looking back to the occasion of discovering that persons with his stigma are human beings like everyone else, the individual may bring to bear a later occasion when his pre-stigma friends imputed un-humanness to those he had by then learned to see as full-fledged persons like himself. Thus, in reviewing her experience as a circus worker, a young girl sees first that she had learned her fellow-workers are not freaks, and second that her pre-circus friends fear for her having to travel in a bus along with other members of the troupe.[81]

Another turning point—retrospectively if not originally—is the isolating, incapacitating experience, often a period of hospitalization, which comes later to be seen as the time when the individual was able to think through his problem, learn about himself, sort out his situation, and arrive at a new understanding of what is important and worth seeking in life.

It should be added that not only are personal experiences retrospectively identified as turning points, but experiences once removed may be employed in this way. For example, a reading of the literature of the group may itself provide an experience felt and claimed as reorganizing:

> I do not think it is claiming too much to say that *Uncle Tom's Cabin* was a fair and truthful panorama of slavery; however that may be, it opened my eyes as to who and what I was and what my country considered me; in fact, it gave me my bearing.[82]

[80] Carling, *op. cit.*, p. 21.
[81] C. Clausen, *I Love You Honey But the Season's Over* (New York: Holt, Rinehart & Winston, 1961), p. 217.
[82] Johnson, *op. cit.*, p. 42. Johnson's novel, like others of its kind, provides a nice instance of myth-making, being a literary organization of many of the crucial moral experiences and crucial turning points retrospectively available to those in a stigmatized category

2. INFORMATION CONTROL and PERSONAL IDENTITY

The Discredited and the Discreditable

When there is a discrepancy between an individual's actual social identity and his virtual one, it is possible for this fact to be known to us before we normals contact him, or to be quite evident when he presents himself before us. He is a discredited person, and it is mainly he I have been dealing with until now. As suggested, we are likely to give no open recognition to what is discrediting of him, and while this work of careful disattention is being done, the situation can become tense, uncertain, and ambiguous for all participants, especially the stigmatized one.

The cooperation of a stigmatized person with normals in acting as if his known differentness were irrelevant and not attended to is one main possibility in the life of such a person. However, when his differentness is not immediately apparent, and is not known beforehand (or at least known by him to be known to the others), when in fact his is a discreditable, not a discredited, person, then the second main possibility in his life is to be found. The issue is not that of managing tension generated during social contacts, but rather that of managing information about his failing. To display or not to display; to tell or not to tell; to let on or not to let on; to lie or not to lie; and in each case, to whom, how, when, and where. For example, while the mental patient is in the hospital, and when he is with adult members of his own family, he is faced with being treated tactfully as if he were sane when there is known to be some doubt, even though he may not have any; or he is treated as insane, when he knows this is not just. But for the ex-mental patient the problem can be quite different; it is not that he must face prejudice against himself, but rather that he must face unwitting acceptance of himself by individuals who are prejudiced against persons of the kind he can be revealed to be. Wherever he goes his behavior will falsely confirm for the other that they are in the company of what in effect they demand but may discover they haven't obtained, namely, a mentally untainted person like themselves. By intention or in effect the ex-mental patient conceals information about his real social identity, receiving and accepting treatment based on false suppositions concerning himself. It is this second general issue, the management of undisclosed discrediting information about self, that I am focusing on in these notes, in brief, "passing." The concealment of creditable facts—reverse passing—of course occurs, but is not relevant here.[1]

[1] For one instance of reverse passing, see "H. E. R. Cules," "Ghost-Writer and Failure," in P. Toynbee, ed., *Underdogs* (London: Weidenfeld and Nicolson, 1961), Chap. 2, pp. 30-39. There are many other examples. I knew a physician who was careful to refrain from using external symbols of her status, such as car-license tags, her only evidence of profession being an identification carried in her wallet. When faced with a public accident in which medical service was already being rendered

Social Information

The information of most relevance in the study of stigma has certain properties. It is information about an individual. It is about his more or less abiding characteristics, as opposed to the moods, feelings, or intents that he might have at a particular moment.[2] The information, as well as the sign through which it is conveyed, is reflexive and embodied; that is, it is conveyed by the very person it is about, and conveyed through bodily expression in the immediate presence of those who receive the expression. Information possessing all of these properties I will here call "social." Some signs that convey social information may be frequently and steadily available, and routinely sought and received; these signs may be called "symbols."

The social information conveyed by any particular symbol may merely confirm what other signs tell us about the individual, filling out our image of him in a redundant and unproblematic way. Some lapel buttons, attesting to social club membership, are examples, as are male wedding rings in some contexts. However, the social information conveyed by a symbol can establish a special claim to prestige, honor, or desirable class position—a claim that might not otherwise be presented or, if otherwise presented, then not automatically granted. Such a sign is popularly called a "status symbol," although the term "prestige symbol" might be more accurate, the former term being more suitably employed when a well-organized social position of some kind is the referent. Prestige symbols can be contrasted to *stigma symbols*, namely, signs which are especially effective in drawing attention to a debasing identity discrep-

---

the victim, or in which the victim was past helping, she would, upon examining the victim at a distance from the circle around him, quietly go her way without announcing her competence. In these situations she was what might be called a female impersonator.

[2] The difference between mood information and other kinds of information is treated in G. Stone, "Appearance and the Self," in A. Rose, *Human Behavior and Social Processes* (Boston: Houghton Mifflin, 1962), pp. 86-118. See also E. Goffman, *The Presentation of Self in Everyday Life* (New York: Doubleday & Co., Anchor Books, 1959), pp. 24-25.

ancy, breaking up what would otherwise be a coherent overall picture, with a consequent reduction in our valuation of the individual. The shaved head of female collaborators in World War II is an example, as is an habitual solecism through which someone affecting middle class manner and dress repeatedly employs a word incorrectly or repeatedly mispronounces it.

In addition to prestige symbols and stigma symbols, one further possibility is to be found, namely, a sign that tends—in fact or hope—to break up an otherwise coherent picture but in this case in a positive direction desired by the actor, not so much establishing a new claim as throwing severe doubt on the validity of the virtual one. I shall refer here to *disidentifiers*. One example is the "good English" of an educated northern Negro visiting the South;[3] another is the turban and mustache affected by some urban lower class Negroes.[4] A study of illiterates provides another illustration:

> Therefore, when goal orientation is pronounced or imperative and there exists a high probability that definition as illiterate is a bar to the achievement of the goal, the illiterate is likely to try to "pass" as literate. . . . The popularity in the group studied of windowpane lenses with heavy horn frames ("bop glasses") may be viewed as an attempt to emulate the stereotype of the businessman-teacher-young intellectual and especially the high status jazz musician.[5]

A New York specialist in the arts of vagrancy provides still another illustration:

> After seven-thirty in the evening, in order to read a book in Grand Central or Penn Station, a person either has to wear horn-rimmed glasses or look exceptionally prosperous. Anyone else is apt to come under surveillance. On the other hand, newspaper readers never seem to attract attention and even the seediest vagrant can sit in

---

[3] G. J. Fleming, "My Most Humiliating Jim Crow Experience," *Negro Digest* (June 1954), 67-68.
[4] B. Wolfe, "Ecstatic in Blackface," *Modern Review*, III (1950), 204.
[5] Freeman and Kasenbaum, *op. cit.*, p. 372.

Grand Central all night without being molested if he continues to read a paper.[6]

Note that in this discussion of prestige symbols, stigma symbols, and disidentifiers, signs have been considered which routinely convey social information. These symbols must be distinguished from fugitive signs that have not been institutionalized as information carriers. When such signs make claims to prestige, one can call them points; when they discredit tacit claims, one can call them slips.

Some signs carrying social information, being present, first of all, for other reasons, have only an overlay of informational function. There are stigma symbols that provide examples: the wrist markings which disclose that an individual has attempted suicide; the arm pock marks of drug addicts; the handcuffed wrists of convicts in transit;[7] or black eyes when worn in public by females, as a writer on prostitution suggests:

> "Outside [the prison where she now is] I'd be in the soup with it. Well, you know how it is: the law sees a chick with a shiner figures she's up to something. Bull figures maybe in the life. Next thing trails her around. Then maybe bang! busted." [8]

Other signs are designed by man solely for the purpose of conveying social information, as in the case of insignia of military rank. It should be added that the significance of the underlay of a sign can become reduced over time, becoming, at the extreme, merely vestigial, even while the informational function of the activity remains constant or increases in importance. Further, a sign that appears to be present for non-informational reasons may sometimes be manufactured with malice aforethought solely because of its informing function, as when dueling scars were carefully planned and inflicted.

[6] E. Love, *Subways Are for Sleeping* (New York: Harcourt, Brace & World, 1957), p. 28.
[7] A. Heckstall-Smith, *Eighteen Months* (London: Allan Wingate, 1954), p. 43.
[8] T. Rubin, *In the Life* (New York: The Macmillan Company, 1961), p. 69.

Signs conveying social information vary according to whether or not they are congenital, and, if not, whether, once employed, they become a permanent part of the person. (Skin color is congenital; a brand mark or maiming is permanent but not congenital; a convict's head-shave is neither congenital nor permanent.) More important, impermanent signs solely employed to convey social information may or may not be employed against the will of the informant; when they are, they tend to be stigma symbols.[9] Later it will be necessary to consider stigma symbols that are voluntarily employed.

It is possible for signs which mean one thing to one group to mean something else to another group, the same category being designated but differently characterized. For example, the shoulder patches that prison officials require escape-prone prisoners to wear[10] can come to mean one thing to guards, in general negative, while being a mark of pride for the wearer relative to his fellow prisoners. The uniform of an officer may be a matter of pride to some, to be worn on every possible occasion; for other officers, weekends may represent a time when they can exercise

[9] In his *American Notes*, written on the basis of his 1842 trip, Dickens records in his chapter on slavery some pages of quotations from local newspapers regarding lost and found slaves. The identifications contained in these advertisements provide a full range of identifying signs. First, there are relatively stable features of the body that in context can incidentally provide partial or full positive identification: age, sex, and scarrings (these resulting from shot and knife wounds, from accidents, and from lashings). Self-admitted name is also provided, though usually, of course, only the first name. Finally, stigma symbols are often cited, notably branded initials and cropped ears. These symbols communicate the social identity of slave but, unlike iron bands around the neck or leg, also communicate something more narrow than that, namely, ownership by a particular master. Authorities then had two concerns about an apprehended Negro: whether or not he was a runaway slave, and, if he was, to whom did he belong.

[10] See G. Dendrickson and F. Thomas, *The Truth About Dartmoor* (London: Victor Gollancz, 1954), p. 55, and F. Norman, *Bang to Rights* (London: Secker and Warburg, 1958), p. 125. The use of this type of symbol is well presented in E. Kogon, *The Theory and Practice of Hell* (New York: Berkley Publishing Corp., n.d.), pp. 41-42, where he specifies the markings used in concentration camps to identify differentially political prisoners, second offenders, criminals, Jehovah's Witnesses, "shiftless elements," Gypsies, Jews, "race defilers," foreign nationals (according to nation), feeble-minded, and so forth. Slaves on the Roman slave market also were often labeled as to nationality; see M. Gordon, "The Nationality of Slaves Under the Early Roman Empire," in M. I. Finley, ed., *Slavery in Classical Antiquity* (Cambridge: Heffer, 1960), p. 171.

their choice and wear mufti, passing as civilians. Similarly, while the obligation to wear the school cap in town may be seen as a privilege by some boys, as will the obligation to wear a uniform on leave by "other ranks," still there will be wearers who feel that the social information conveyed thereby is a means of ensuring control and discipline over them when they are off duty and off the premises.[11] So, too, during the eighteen hundreds in California, the absence of a pigtail (queue) on a Chinese man signified for Occidentals a degree of acculturation, but to fellow-Chinese a question would be raised as to respectability—specifically, whether or not the individual had served a term in prison where cutting off of the queue was obligatory; loss of queue was for a time, then, very strongly resisted.[12]

Signs carrying social information vary of course as to reliability. Distended capillaries on the cheek and nose, sometimes called "venous stigmata" with more aptness than meant, can be and are taken as indicating alcoholic excess. However, teetotalers can exhibit the same symbol for other physiological reasons, thereby giving rise to suspicions about themselves which aren't justified, but with which they must deal nonetheless.

A final point about social information must be raised; it has to do with the informing character of the "with" relationship in our society. To be "with" someone is to arrive at a social occasion in his company, walk with him down a street, be a member of his party in a restaurant, and so forth. The issue is that in certain circumstances the social identity of those an individual is with can be used as a source of information concerning his own social identity, the assumption being that he is what the others are. The extreme, perhaps, is the situation in criminal circles: a person wanted for arrest can legally contaminate anyone he is seen with, subjecting them to arrest on suspicion. (A

---

[11] T. H. Pear, *Personality, Appearance and Speech* (London: George Allen and Unwin, 1957), p. 58.

[12] A. McLeod, *Pigtails and Gold Dust* (Caldwell, Idaho: Caxton Printers, 1947); p. 28. At times religious-historical significance was also attached to wearing the queue; see *ibid.*, p. 204.

person for whom there is a warrant is therefore said "to have smallpox," and his criminal disease is said to be "catching.")[13] In any case, an analysis of how people manage the information they convey about themselves will have to consider how they deal with the contingencies of being seen "with" particular others.

Visibility

Traditionally, the question of passing has raised the issue of the "visibility" of a particular stigma, that is, how well or how badly the stigma is adapted to provide means of communicating that the individual possesses it. For example, ex-mental patients and expectant unmarried fathers are similar in that their failing is not readily visible; the blind, however, are easily seen. Visibility, of course, is a crucial factor. That which can be told about an individual's social identity at all times during his daily round and by all persons he encounters therein will be of great importance to him. The consequence of a presentation that is perforce made to the public at large may be small in particular contacts, but in every contact there will be some consequences, which, taken together, can be immense. Further, routinely available information about him is the base from which he must begin when deciding what tack to take in regard to whatever stigma he possesses. Thus, any change in the way the individual must always and everywhere present himself will for these very reasons be fateful—this presumably providing the Greeks with the idea of stigma in the first place.

Since it is through our sense of sight that the stigma of others most frequently becomes evident, the term visibility is perhaps not too misleading. Actually, the more general term, "perceptibility" would be more accurate, and "evidentness" more accurate still. A stammer, after all, is a very "visible" defect, but in the first instance because of sound, not sight. Before the concept of visibility can be safely used even in this corrected version,

[13] See D. Maurer, *The Big Con* (New York: Pocket Books, 1949), p. 298.

however, it must be distinguished from three other notions that are often confused with it.

First, the visibility of a stigma must be distinguished from its "known-about-ness." When an individual's stigma is very visible, his merely contacting others will cause his stigma to be known about. But whether others know about the individual's stigma will depend on another factor in addition to its current visibility, namely, whether or not they have previous knowledge about him—and this can be based on gossip about him or a previous contact with him during which his stigma was visible.

Secondly, visibility must be distinguished from one of its particular bases, namely, obtrusiveness. When a stigma is immediately perceivable, the issue still remains as to how much it interferes with the flow of interaction. For example, at a business meeting a participant in a wheelchair is certainly seen to be in a wheelchair, but around the conference table his failing can become relatively easy to disattend. On the other hand, a participant with a speech impediment, who in many ways is much less handicapped than someone in a wheelchair, can hardly open his mouth without destroying any unconcern that may have arisen concerning his failing, and he will continue to introduce uneasiness each time thereafter that he speaks. The very mechanics of spoken encounters constantly redirect attention to the defect, constantly making demands for clear and rapid messages that must constantly be defaulted. It may be added that the same failing can have different expressions, each with a different degree of obtrusiveness. For example, a blind person with a white cane gives quite visible evidence that he is blind; but this stigma symbol, once noted, can sometimes be disattended, along with what it signifies. But the blind person's failure to direct his face to the eyes of his co-participants is an event that repeatedly violates communication etiquette and repeatedly disrupts the feed-back mechanics of spoken interaction.

Thirdly, the visibility of a stigma (as well as its obtrusiveness) must be disentangled from certain possibilities of what can be called its "perceived focus." We normals develop conceptions.

whether objectively grounded or not, as to the sphere of life-activity for which an individual's particular stigma primarily disqualifies him. Ugliness, for example, has its initial and prime effect during social situations, threatening the pleasure we might otherwise take in the company of its possessor. We perceive, however, that his condition ought to have no effect on his competency in solitary tasks, although of course we may discriminate against him here simply because of the feelings we have about looking at him. Ugliness, then, is a stigma that is focused in social situations. Other stigmas, such as a diabetic condition,[14] are felt to have no initial effect on the individual's qualifications for face-to-face interaction; they lead us first to discriminate in such matters as job allocation, and affect immediate social interaction only, for example, because the stigmatized individual may have attempted to keep his differentness a secret and feels unsure about being able to do so, or because the others present know about his condition and are making a painful effort not to allude to it. Many other stigmas fall in between these two extremes regarding focus, being perceived to have a broad initial effect in many different areas of life. For example, a person with cerebral palsy may not only be seen as burdensome in face-to-face communication, but may also induce the feeling that he is questionable as a solitary task performer.

The question of visibility, then, must be distinguished from some other issues: the known-about-ness of the attribute, its obtrusiveness, and its perceived focus. This still leaves unconsidered the tacit assumption that somehow the public at large will be engaged in the viewing. But as we shall see, specialists at uncovering identity can be involved, and their training may allow them to be immediately struck by something that is invisible to the laity. A physician who meets on the street a man with dull red discoloration of the cornea and notched teeth is meeting someone who openly displays two of Hutchinson's signs and is likely to be syphilitic. Others present, however, being

[14] "A Reluctant Pensioner," "Unemployed Diabetic," in Toynbee, *op. cit.*, Chap. 9, pp. 132-146.

medically blind, will see no evil. In general, then, the decoding capacity of the audience must be specified before one can speak of degree of visibility.

Personal Identity

In order systematically to consider the situation of the discreditable person and his problem of concealment and disclosure, it was necessary first to examine the character of social information and of visibility. Before proceeding it will be necessary to consider, and at considerable length, still another factor, that of identification—in the criminological and not the psychological sense.

So far, the analysis of social interaction between the stigmatized and the normal has not required that those involved in the mixed contact know one another "personally" before the interaction begins. This seems reasonable. Stigma management is an offshoot of something basic in society, the stereotyping or "profiling" of our normative expectations regarding conduct and character; stereotyping is classically reserved for customers, orientals, and motorists, that is, persons who fall into very broad categories and who may be passing strangers to us.

There is a popular notion that although impersonal contacts between strangers are particularly subject to stereotypical responses, as persons come to be on closer terms with each other this categoric approach recedes and gradually sympathy, understanding, and a realistic assessment of personal qualities take its place.[15] While a blemish such as a facial disfigurement might put off a stranger, intimates presumably would not be put off by such matters. The area of stigma management, then, might be seen as something that pertains mainly to public life, to contact between strangers or mere acquaintances, to one end of a continuum whose other pole is intimacy.

The idea of such a continuum no doubt has some validity. For

[15] A traditional statement of this theme may be found in N. S. Shaler, *The Neighbor* (Boston: Houghton Mifflin, 1904).

example, it has been shown that in addition to techniques for handling strangers, the physically handicapped may develop special techniques for moving past the initial tactfulness and distance they are likely to receive; they may attempt to move on to a more "personal" plane where in fact their defect will cease to be a crucial factor—an arduous process Fred Davis calls "breaking through." [16] Further, those with a bodily stigma report that, within certain limits, normals with whom they have repeated dealings will gradually come to be less put off by the disability, so that something like a daily round of normalization may hopefully develop. A blind person's round may be cited:

> There are now barbershops where I am received with some of the calmness of old, of course, and hotels, restaurants, and public buildings which I can enter without engendering a feeling that something is going to happen; a few trolley motormen and bus drivers now merely wish me Good Morning when I get on with my dog, and a few waiters I know serve me with traditional unconcern. Naturally, the immediate circle of my family has long since ceased doing any unnecessary worrying about me, and so have most of my intimate friends. To that extent I have made a dent in the education of the world.[17]

The same sheltering can presumably occur in regard to whole categories of the stigmatized: the service shops which are sometimes found in the immediate neighborhood of mental hospitals may become places with high tolerance for psychotic behavior; the neighborhoods around some medical hospitals develop a capacity for calm treatment of the facially disfigured who are undergoing skin grafting; the town in which a seeing-eye school is located learns to countenance blind students engaged in the act of holding a harness attached to a human instructor all the while offering him periodic words of canine encouragement.[18]

In spite of this evidence for everyday beliefs about stigma and

---

[16] Davis, *op. cit.*, pp. 127-128.
[17] Chevigny, *op. cit.*, pp. 75-76.
[18] Keitlen, *op. cit.*, p. 85.

familiarity, one must go on to see that familiarity need not reduce contempt.[19] For example, normals who live adjacent to settlements of the tribally stigmatized often manage quite handily to sustain their prejudices. It is more important here, however, to see that the various consequences of making a whole array of virtual assumptions about an individual are clearly present in our dealings with persons with whom we have had a long-standing, intimate, exclusive relationship. In our society, to speak of a woman as one's wife is to place this person in a category of which there can be only one current member, yet a category is nonetheless involved, and she is merely a member of it. Unique, historically entangled features are likely to tint the edges of our relation to this person; still, at the center is a full array of socially standardized anticipations that we have regarding her conduct and nature as an instance of the category "wife," for example, that she will look after the house, entertain our friends, and be able to bear children. She will be a good or a bad wife, and be this relative to standard expectations, ones that other husbands in our group have about their wives too. (Surely it is scandalous to speak of marriage as a particularistic relationship.) Thus, whether we interact with strangers or intimates, we will find that the finger tips of society have reached bluntly into the contact, even here putting us in our place.

There are sure to be cases where those who are not required to share the individual's stigma or spend much time exerting tact and care in regard to it may find it easier to accept him, just because of this, than do those who are obliged to be in full-time contact with him.

When one moves from a consideration of discredited persons to discreditable ones, much additional evidence is found that the individual's intimates as well as his strangers will be put off by his stigma. For one thing, the individual's intimates can become just the persons from whom he is most concerned with

---

[19] For evidence that normal children at a summer camp do not come with time to accept physically handicapped fellow-members more readily, see Richardson, *op. cit.*, p. 7.

concealing something shameful; the situation of homosexuals provides an illustration:

> Although it is usual for a homosexual to protest that his deviation is not a disease, it is noteworthy that if he consults anyone at all, it is more likely to be a doctor than anyone else. But it is not likely to be his own family doctor. Most of the contacts were anxious to keep their homosexuality hidden from their family. Even some of those who behave fairly openly in public are most careful to avoid arousing suspicions in the family circle.[20]

Further, while one parent in a family may share a dark secret about, and with, the other, the children of the house may be considered not only unsafe receptacles for the information but also of such tender nature as to be seriously damaged by the knowledge. The case of the mentally hospitalized parent is an example:

> In interpreting the father's illness to younger children, almost all the mothers attempt to follow a course of concealment. The child is told either that his father is in a hospital (without further explanation) or that he is in the hospital suffering from a physical ailment (he has a toothache, or trouble with his leg, or a tummy ache, or a headache).[21]

> [Wife of mental patient] "I live in a horror—a perfect horror—that some people will make a crack about it to Jim (child). . . ."[22]

One may add that there are some stigmas that are so easily concealed that they figure very little in the individual's relation to strangers and mere acquaintances, having their effect chiefly upon intimates—frigidity, impotence, and sterility being good examples. Thus, in trying to account for the fact that alcoholism

---

[20] G. Westwood, *A Minority* (London: Longmans, Green & Company, 1960), p. 40.

[21] M. R. Yarrow, J. A. Clausen, and P. R. Robbins, "The Social Meaning of Mental Illness," *Journal of Social Issues*, XI (1955), 40-41. This paper provides much useful material on stigma management.

[22] *Ibid.*, p. 34.

does not seem to disqualify a man from embarking upon marriage, one student suggests that:

> It is also possible that the circumstances of courtship or the pattern of the drinking may so lower the visibility of alcoholism that it is not a factor in mate selection. The more intimate interaction of marriage may then bring out the problem in a form recognizable to the spouse.[23]

Moreover, intimates can come to play a special role in the discreditable person's management of social situations, so that even where their acceptance of him is not influenced by his stigma, their duties will be.

Instead, then, of thinking of a continuum of relationships, with categoric and concealing treatment at one end and particularistic, open treatment at the other, it might be better to think of various structures in which contact occurs and is stabilized—public streets and their strangers, perfunctory service relations, the workplace, the neighborhood, the domestic scene—and to see that in each case characteristic discrepancies are likely to occur between virtual and actual social identity, and characteristic efforts are made to manage the situation.

And yet, the whole problem of managing stigma is influenced by the issue of whether or not the stigmatized person is known to us personally. To attempt to describe just what this influence is, however, requires the clear formulation of an additional concept, *personal identity*.[24]

---

[23] E. Lemert, "The Occurrence and Sequence of Events in the Adjustment of Families to Alcoholism," *Quarterly Journal of Studies on Alcohol*, XXI (1960), 683.

[24] A distinction between personal identity and role identity is presented clearly in R. Sommer, H. Osmond, and L. Pancyr, "Problems of Recognition and Identity," *International Journal of Parapsychology*, II (1960), 99-119, where the problem is posed as to how one establishes either or disproves either. See also Goffman, *The Presentation of Self in Everyday Life, op. cit.*, p. 60. The idea of personal identity is also used by C. Rolph, *Personal Identity* (London: Michael Joseph, 1957), and by E. Schachtel, "On Alienated Concepts of Identity," *American Journal of Psychoanalysis*, XXI (1961), 120-121, under the title, "paper identity." The concept of legal or jural identity corresponds closely to personal identity except that (as Harvey Sacks has informed me) there are some situations, as in adoptions, where the legal identity of an individual may be changed.

It is well appreciated that in small, long-standing social circles each member comes to be known to the others as a "unique" person. The term unique is subject to pressure by maiden social scientists who would make something warm and creative out of it, a something not to be further broken down, at least by sociologists; nonetheless, the term does involve some relevant ideas.

One idea involved in the notion of "uniqueness" of an individual is that of a "positive mark" or "identity peg," for example, the photographic image of the individual in others' minds, or the knowledge of his special place in a particular kinship network. An interesting comparative case is that of the Tuareg of West Africa whose males cover their faces leaving only a small slit to see out of; here, apparently, the face as an anchorage for personal identification is replaced by body appearance and physical style.[25] Only one person at a time can be fitted to the image I am here discussing, and he who qualified in the past is the self-same person who qualifies in the present and will do so in the future. Note that items such as fingerprints which are the most effective means of rendering individuals identifiably different are also items in terms of which they are essentially similar.

A second idea is that, while most particular facts about an individual will be true of others too, the full set of facts known about an intimate is not found to hold, as a combination, for any other person in the world, this adding a means by which he can be positively distinguished from everyone else. Sometimes this complex of information is name-bound, as in the case of a police dossier; sometimes it is body-bound, as when we come to know the pattern of behavior of someone whose face we know but whose name we do not know; often the information is bound both to name and body.

A third idea is that what distinguishes an individual from all others is the core of his being, a general and central aspect of him, making him different through and through, not merely identifiably different, from those who are most like him.

[25] I am here indebted to an unpublished paper by Robert Murphy, "On Social Distance and the Veil."

By *personal identity*, I have in mind only the first two ideas—positive marks or identity pegs, and the unique combination of life history items that comes to be attached to the individual with the help of these pegs for his identity. Personal identity, then, has to do with the assumption that the individual can be differentiated from all others and that around this means of differentiation a single continuous record of social facts can be attached, entangled, like candy floss, becoming then the sticky substance to which still other biographical facts can be attached. What is difficult to appreciate is that personal identity can and does play a structured, routine, standardized role in social organization just because of its one-of-a-kind quality.

The process of personal identification can be seen at work clearly if one takes as a point of reference not a small group but a large impersonal organization, such as a state government. It is now standard organizational practice that a means of positive identification for every individual to be dealt with is officially recorded, that is, a set of marks is used that distinguishes the person so marked from all other individuals. As suggested, the choice of mark is itself quite standard: unchanging biological attributes such as handwriting or photographically attested appearance; permanently recordable items such as birth certificate, name, and serial number. Recently, through the use of computer analysis, experimental progress has been made in using speech and handwriting qualities as identity pegs, thus exploiting a minor expressive feature of behavior much as specialists do in "authenticating" paintings. More important, the Social Security Act of 1935 in America ensures that almost every employee will have a unique registration number to which can be affixed a lifelong record of employment, a scheme of identification which has already worked considerable hardship on our criminal classes. In any case, once an identity peg has been made ready, material, if and when available, can be hung on it; a dossier can be developed, usually contained and filed in a manila folder. One can expect that personal identification of its citizens by the state will increase, even as devices are refined for making the record of a particular individual more easily available to authorized persons and more inclusive of social facts concerning him, for example, receipt of dividend payments.

There is considerable popular interest in the efforts of harried persons to acquire a personal identity not their "own" or to disengage themselves from the one that was originally theirs, as in efforts to scar finger tips or to destroy public birth certificate records. In actual cases, personal name is usually the issue, because of all identity pegs it seems to be the one most generally employed and at the same time the one that is in certain ways easiest to tamper with. The respectable and legally advisable way of changing one's name is by a documented act, the record of which is available in a public file. A single continuity is thus preserved in spite of apparent diversity.[26] This is the case, for example, when a woman changes her last name through the act of marriage. In the entertainment world it is common for a performer to change his name, but here, too, a record of the previous name is likely to be available, and even widely known, as is also the case with pen-named authors. Occupations where a change in name can occur without being officially recorded, such as those of prostitute, criminal, and revolutionary, are not "legitimate" trades. A remaining case is that of the Catholic clerical orders. Wherever an occupation carries with it a change in name, recorded or not, one can be sure that an important breach is involved between the individual and his old world.

It should be stated that some name changes, such as those employed by draft dodgers and motel guests, are specifically oriented to the legal aspects of personal identification, while other changes, such as ones employed by ethnics, are oriented to the issue of social identity. One student implies that some professional entertainers have the distinction of qualifying on both counts:

> The average chorus girl changes her name almost as frequently as her coiffure to accord with current theatrical popularity, show-

---
[26] See Rolph, *Personal Identity, op. cit.*, pp. 14-16.

business superstitions, or, in some cases, to avoid payment of Equity dues.[27]

I might add that professional criminals employ two special types of re-naming: aliases, used very temporarily, although often repeatedly, to avoid personal identification; "monikers," namely, nicknames given in the criminal community and retained for life, but used only by and to members of the community or the wise.

A name, then, is a very common but not very reliable way of fixing identity. When a court of law must deal with someone who has every motivation to misrepresent himself, it is understandable that other positive marks will be sought. The English case may be cited:

... personal identity is proved in courts of law, not by reference to names, not even mainly by direct testimony, but "presumptively" by evidence of similarities or differences in personal characteristics.[28]

The question of social information must now be raised again. The embodied signs previously considered, whether of prestige or stigma, pertain to social identity. Clearly all of these must be distinguished from the *documentation* that individuals carry around with them purportedly establishing personal identity. These documents have come to be widely used in Britain and America by natives as well as foreigners. Registration cards and drivers' licenses (containing fingerprints, signatures, and sometimes photographs) are felt to be necessary.[29] Along with these self-identifications, the individual may carry documentation of age (in the case of youths who wish to frequent gambling establishments or to be served liquor), a license to engage in protected or dangerous trades, permission to be away from barracks, and so

---

[27] A. Hartman, "Criminal Aliases: A Psychological Study," *Journal of Psychology*, XXXII (1951), 53.

[28] Rolph, *Personal Identity, op. cit.*, p. 18.

[29] In Britain, currently, citizens are not obliged to carry identification documents, although aliens and motorists are; also, under certain circumstances, British citizens can decline to tell policemen who they are. See *ibid.*, pp. 12-13.

forth. This information is often supplemented by family pictures, evidence of past military service, and even photostatic copies of college certificates. Recently, information about the bearer's medical status has also appeared, and its general use advocated:

> Medical identity cards for all are being considered by the Ministry of Health. People would be asked to carry them always.
>
> The card would contain details such as vaccinations, owner's blood group, and of any disease, such as hemophilia, that should be known immediately if the person is involved in an accident.
>
> One of the aims is to help quick treatment in an emergency and to avoid the dangers of injecting people with vaccine to which they might be allergic.[30]

It may be added that there appears to be an increasing number of work establishments which require the individual to wear, and if not wear then possess on person, employee identification cards with photographs.

The whole point of these various identification devices is, of course, that they allow no innocent error or ambiguity, transforming what would be merely a questionable use of socially informing symbols into clear-cut forgery or illegal possession; therefore the term identity document might be more accurate than identity symbol. (Compare, for example, the relatively loose basis for identification of Jewish identity through appearance, gesture, and voice.)[31] Incidentally, this documentation and the social facts attached thereto are often presented only in special situations to those specially authorized to check up on identity, unlike prestige and stigma symbols, which are more likely to be available to the public at large.

Because information about personal identity often is of the kind that can be strictly documented, it can be used to safeguard against potential misrepresentation of social identity.

[30] Reported in *The San Francisco Chronicle*, April 14, 1963, and attributed to *The London Times*.
[31] L. Savitz and R. Tomasson, "The Identifiability of Jews," *American Journal of Sociology*, LXIV (1959), 468-475.

Thus, army personnel may be required to carry identity documents validating the potentially false claims of their uniform and its insignia. The student's personal identification card assures the librarian that he is vested with the right to borrow library books or to enter the stacks, just as his driver's license can attest that he is of legal age for drinking in commercial establishments. So, too, credit cards attest on the surface to personal identity, useful in deciding whether to give or to withhold credit, but in addition attest to the individual's being of a social category to warrant such accrediting. A man proves he is Dr. Hiram Smith to prove he is a doctor, perhaps rarely showing he is a doctor to prove he is Hiram Smith. Similarly, individuals excluded from some hotels on the basis of their ethnicity may have been ethnically identified through their names, so that here, too, an item of personal biography is exploited for categoric reasons.

In general, then, biography attached to documented identity can place clear limitations on the way in which an individual can elect to present himself; the situation of some British ex-mental patients who cannot pass as ordinary job applicants at the Employment Exchange because their National Insurance cards have unstamped gaps, provides an illustration.[32] I might add that the act of concealing personal identity can itself carry implications regarding social category: the sun glasses that celebrities employ to conceal their personal identity presumably reveal, or did for a time, a social categorization of someone who wants to be incognito and would otherwise be recognized.

Once the difference between social symbols and identity documents is perceived, one can go on to look at the special position of oral statements which attest linguistically, not merely expressively, to social and personal identity. Where an individual has insufficient documentation to receive a desired service, he can be seen to attempt use of oral testaments in its place. Groups and societies differ, of course, in their beliefs as to how much

[32] E. Mills, *Living with Mental Illness: A Study in East London* (London: Routledge & Kegan Paul Ltd., 1962), p. 112.

identity testament is appropriate in roughly equivalent social situations. Thus, an Indian writer suggests:

> In our society a man is always what his designation makes him, therefore we are very punctilious in giving it. At parties in Delhi I see people adding it themselves when the introducers omit to announce it. One day, at the house of a foreign diplomat in Delhi, a young man was introduced to me without his official position being mentioned. He immediately bowed and added, "Of the X-Ministry, and what Department are you from?" When I replied that I belonged to none, he seemed to be as much surprised by the fact that I had been invited there at all as by my not having a designation.[33]

Biography

Whether an individual's biographical life line is sustained in the minds of his intimates or in the personnel files of an organization, and whether the documentation of his personal identity is carried on his person or stored in files, he is an entity about which a record can be built up—a copybook has been made ready for him to blot. He is anchored as an object for biography.[34]

While the biography has been used by social scientists, especially in the form of a career life history, little attention has been given to the general properties of the concept, except in noting that biographies are very subject to retrospective construction. Social role as a concept and as a formal element of social organization has been thoroughly examined, but biography has not.

The first point to note about biographies is that we assume that an individual can really have only one of them, this being guaranteed by the laws of physics rather than those of society. Anything and everything an individual has done and can actually do is understood to be containable within his biography, as the Jekyll-Hyde theme illustrates, even if we have to hire a

---

[33] C. Chaudhuri, *A Passage to England* (London: Macmillan & Company, 1959), p. 92.
[34] I am very much indebted here to Harold Garfinkel, who introduced me to the term "biography" as used in this book.

biography specialist, a private detective, to fill in the missing facts and connect the discovered ones for us. No matter how big a scoundrel a man is, no matter how false, secretive, or disjointed his existence, or how governed by fits, starts, and reversals, the true facts of his activity cannot be contradictory or unconnected with each other. Note that this embracing singleness of life line is in sharp contrast to the multiplicity of selves one finds in the individual in looking at him from the perspective of social role, where, if role and audience segregation is well managed, he can quite handily sustain different selves and can to a degree claim to be no longer something he was.

Given these assumptions about the nature of personal identity, a factor emerges that will be relevant for this report: degree of "informational connectedness." Given the important social facts about a person, the kind of facts reported in his obituary, how close to each other or how distant is a given pair of them as measured by the frequency with which those who know either fact will also know the other? More generally, given the body of important social facts about the individual, in what degree do those who know some know many?

Social misrepresentation is to be distinguished from personal misrepresentation; an upper middle class businessman who takes off for a lost weekend by "dressing down" and going to a cheap summer resort misrepresents himself in the first way; when he registers in a motel as Mr. Smith he misrepresents himself in the second way. And whether social or personal identity is involved, one can distinguish representation aimed at proving one is what one isn't, from representation aimed at proving one is not what one is.

In general, norms regarding social identity, as earlier implied, pertain to the kinds of role repertoires or profiles we feel it permissible for any given individual to sustain—"social personality," as Lloyd Warner used to say.[35] We do not expect a pool shark to be either a woman or a classical scholar, but we are not sur-

---

[35] W. L. Warner, "The Society, the Individual, and His Mental Disorder," *American Journal of Psychiatry*, XCIV (1937), 278-279.

prised or embarrassed by the fact that he is also a working class Italian or an urban Negro. Norms regarding *personal* identity, however, pertain not to ranges of permissible combinations of social attributes but rather to the kind of information control the individual can appropriately exert. For the individual to have had what is called a shady past is an issue regarding his social identity; the way he handles information about this past is a question of personal identification. Possession of a strange past (not strange in itself, of course, but strange for someone of the individual's current social identity) is one kind of impropriety; for the possessor to live out a life before those who are ignorant of this past and not informed about it by him can be a very different kind of impropriety, the first having to do with our rules regarding social identity, the second with those regarding personal identity.

Apparently in middle class circles today, the more there is about the individual that deviates in an undesirable direction from what might have been expected to be true of him, the more he is obliged to volunteer information about himself, even though the cost to him of candor may have increased proportionately. (On the other hand, the concealment by one individual of something he should have revealed about himself does not give us the right to ask him the kind of question that will force him to disclose the facts or tell a knowing lie. When we do ask such a question a double embarrassment results, ours for being tactless, his for what he has concealed. He can also feel badly about having put us in a position to feel guilty about embarrassing him.) Here, the right to reticence seems earned only by having nothing to hide.[36] It also seems that in order to handle his personal identity it will be necessary for the individual to know to whom he owes much information and to whom he owes very little—even though in all cases he may be obliged to refrain from telling an "outright" lie. By implication it will also be

---

[36] For a sharp contrast, compare the code in the Old West, where apparently one's past and one's original name were defined as rightful private property. See, for example, R. Adams, *The Old-Time Cowboy* (New York: The Macmillan Company, 1961), p. 60.

necessary for him to have a "memory," that is, in this case, an accurate and ready accounting in his own mind regarding the facts of his present and past which he might owe to others.[37]

The bearing of personal identification and social identification upon each other must now be considered, and an attempt made to unravel some of the more apparent intertwinings.

It is plain that in constructing a personal identification of an individual we make use of aspects of his social identity—along with everything else that can be associated with him. It is also plain that being able to identify an individual personally gives us a memory device for organizing and consolidating information regarding his social identity—a process which may subtly alter the meaning of the social characteristics we impute to him.

It can be assumed that the possession of a discreditable secret failing takes on a deeper meaning when the persons to whom the individual has not yet revealed himself are not strangers to him but friends. Discovery prejudices not only the current social situation, but established relationships as well; not only the current image others present have of him, but also the one they will have in the future; not only appearances, but also reputation. The stigma and the effort to conceal it or remedy it become "fixed" as part of personal identity. Hence our increased willingness to chance improper behavior when wearing a mask,[38] or when away from home; hence the willingness of some to publish revelatory material anonymously, or to make a public appearance before a small private audience, the assumption being that the disclosure will not be connected to them personally by the public at large. An instructive example of the latter has recently been reported regarding the Mattachine Society, an organization devoted to presenting and improving the situation of homosexuals, as part of which the Society publishes a journal. Appar-

---

[37] On the social framework for memory in general, see F. C. Bartlett, *Remembering* (Cambridge: Cambridge University Press, 1961).

[38] It is not only bandits and Klansmen who wear masks to avoid recognition. At recent State of Washington crime investigation hearings, ex-dope addicts have been allowed to testify while wearing a sheet over their heads, not only to avoid public identification but also to avoid retaliation.

ently a branch office in a commercial building can be busy with public-oriented efforts, while the officers otherwise conduct themselves so that other tenants in the building remain unaware of what is being undertaken and by whom.[39]

Biographical Others

Personal identity, like social identity, divides up the individual's world of others for him. The division is first between the knowing and the unknowing. The knowing are those who have a personal identification of the individual; they need only see him or hear his name to bring this information into play. The unknowing are those for whom the individual constitutes an utter stranger, someone of whom they have begun no personal biography.

The individual who is known about by others may or may not know that he is known about by them; they in turn may or may not know that he knows or doesn't know of their knowing about him. Further, while believing that they do not know about him, nonetheless he can never be sure. Also, if he knows they know about him, he must, in some measure at least, know about them; but if he does not know that they know about him, he may or may not know about them in regard to other matters.

All of this can be relevant apart from *how much* is or is not known, since the individual's problem in managing his social and personal identity will vary greatly according to whether or not those in his presence know of him, and, if so, whether or not he knows they know of him.

When an individual is among persons for whom he is an utter stranger, and is meaningful only in terms of his immediately apparent social identity, the great contingency for him is whether or not they will begin to build up a personal identification of him (at the least a memory of having seen him in the context conducting himself in a particular way), or whether

[39] J. Stearn, *The Sixth Man* (New York: McFadden Books, 1962), pp. 154-155.

they will refrain altogether from organizing and storing their knowledge about him around a personal identification, this latter being a characteristic of the fully anonymous situation. Note that while public streets in large cities provide anonymous situations for the well behaved, this anonymity is biographical; there is hardly such a thing as complete anonymity regarding social identity. It may be added that every time an individual joins an organization or a community, there is a marked change in the structure of knowledge about him—its distribution and character—and hence a change in the contingencies of information control.[40] For example, every ex-mental patient must face having formed in the hospital some acquaintances who may have to be greeted socially on the outside, leading a third person to ask, "Who was that?" More important, perhaps, he must face the unknown-about knowing, that is, persons who can personally identify him and will know, when he does not know they know, that he is "really" an ex-mental patient.

By the term *cognitive recognition*, I shall refer to the perceptual act of "placing" an individual, whether as having a particular social identity or a particular personal identity. Recognition of social identities is a well-known gate-keeping function of many servers. It is less well known that recognition of personal identities is a formal function in some organizations. In banks, for example, tellers may be expected to acquire this kind of capacity regarding customers. In British criminal circles there is, apparently, an office called "corner-man" whose incumbent takes up a post on the street near the entrance of an illicit business and, by knowing the personal identity of nearly everyone who passes, is able to warn of the approach of a suspicious character.[41]

Within the circle of persons who have biographical information about an individual—who are knowing in regard to him—

---

[40] For one case study in the control of information about self, see J. Henry, "The Formal Structure of a Psychiatric Hospital," *Psychiatry*, XVII (1954), 139-152, especially 149-150.

[41] A description of the functions of the corner-man may be found in J. Phelan, *The Underworld* (London: George G. Harrap & Company, 1953), Chap. 16, pp. 175-186.

there will be a smaller circle of those who are acquainted with him "socially," whether slightly or intimately, and whether as an equal or not. As we say, they not only know "of" or "about" him, they know him "personally" as well. They will have the right and the obligation of exchanging a nod, a greeting, or a chat with him when they find themselves in the same social situation with him, this constituting *social recognition*. Of course, there will be times when an individual extends social recognition to, or receives it from, an individual he does not know personally. In any case, it should be clear that cognitive recognition is simply an act of perception, while social recognition is one individual's part in a communication ceremony.

Social acquaintanceship or personal knowing is necessarily reciprocal, although of course one or even both of the acquainted persons can temporarily forget they are acquainted, just as one or both can be alive to the acquaintanceship but temporarily forgetful of almost everything about the other's personal identity.[42]

For the individual who lives a village life, whether in town or city, there will be few who merely know of him; those that know about him are likely to know him personally. In contrast, by the term "fame" we seem to refer to the possibility that the circle of people who know about a given individual, especially in connection with a rare desirable achievement or possession, can become very wide, and at the same time much wider than the circle of those who know him personally.

The treatment accorded an individual on the basis of his social identity is often accorded with added deference and indulgence to a famed person because of his personal identity. Like a small-town person, he will always be shopping where he is known. The mere fact of being cognitively recognized in public places by strangers can also be a source of satisfaction, as a young actor suggests:

[42] Further treatment of acquaintanceship and types of recognition may be found in E. Goffman, *Behavior in Public Places* (New York: Free Press of Glencoe, 1963), Chap. 7, pp. 112-123.

> When I first became a little well-known and had a day when I was feeling down, I'd actually say to myself, "Well, I think I'll go out for a walk and be recognized." [43]

This kind of promiscuous minor acclaim presumably provides one reason why fame is sought; it also suggests why fame once obtained is sometimes hidden from. The issue is not only the nuisance in being chased by reporters, autograph hunters, and turned heads, but also that a widened range of acts become assimilated to biography as newsworthy events. For a famous person to "get away" where he can "be himself" may mean his finding a community in which there is no biography of him; here his conduct, reflecting merely on his social identity, can have a chance of being of interest to no one. Contrariwise, one aspect of being "on" is acting in a fashion designed to control implications for biography, but doing this in what are ordinarily non-biography creating areas of life.

In the everyday life of an average person there will be long stretches of time when events involving him will be memorable to no one, a technical but not active part of his biography. Only a serious personal accident or the witnessing of a murder will create moments during these dead periods which have a place in the reviews he and others come to make of his past. (An "alibi," in fact, is a presented piece of biography that ordinarily would not have become part of one's active biography at all.) On the other hand, notables who come to have a book-length biography written about them, and especially those such as royalty who are known from the start to be destined for this fate, will find they have experienced few periods of life which are allowed to remain dead, that is, inactively part of their biography.

When considering fame it can be useful and convenient to consider ill-fame or infamy, this arising when there is a circle of persons who know ill of an individual without having met him

---

[43] Anthony Perkins, in L. Ross, "The Player-III," *The New Yorker* (Nov. 4, 1961) 88.

personally. The obvious function of ill-fame is social control, of which two distinct possibilities must be mentioned:

Formal social control is the first. There are functionaries, and circles of functionaries, employed to scan various publics for the presence of identifiable individuals whose record and reputation have made them suspect, or even "wanted" for arrest. For example, during a mental hospital study, I knew a patient who had "town parole" and also a record of having molested very young girls. On entering any of the neighboring movie houses he was likely to be spotted by the manager and made to leave. He was, in short, too ill-famed to attend movies in the neighborhood. Well-known "hoods" have had the same problem, but on a scale larger than could be effected by theater managers.

It is here that one deals with further examples of the occupation of making personal identifications. Floorwalkers in stores, for example, sometimes have extensive records of the appearance of professional shoplifters along with that identity peg called the *modus operandi*. The production of personal identification may in fact be accorded a social occasion of its own, as in the police line-up. Dickens, in describing the social mixing of prisoners and visitors in a London jail, provides another example, called "sitting for one's portrait," whereby a new prisoner was obliged to sit in a chair while the guards gathered and looked at him, fixing his image in their minds so as to be able to spot him later.[44]

Functionaries whose job is to check up on the possible presence of the ill-reputed may operate in the public at large instead of in particular social establishments, as in the case of police detectives who range over a whole city, but do not themselves constitute this public. One is led then to consider a second type of social control based on ill-fame, but this time an informal type of control involving the public at large; and this time the famed can be seen to be in much the same position as the ill-famed.

It is possible for the circle of those who know of an individual

---

[44] *Pickwick Papers*, Vol. III, Chap. 2.

(but are not known by him) to include the public at large, not merely those employed to make identifications. (In fact the terms "fame" and "ill-fame" imply that the citizenry at large must possess an image of the individual.) No doubt the mass media play the central role here, making it possible for a "private" person to be transformed into a "public" figure.

Now it seems the case that the public image of an individual, that is, the image of him available to those who do not know him personally, will necessarily be somewhat different from the image he projects through direct dealings with those who know him personally. Where an individual has a public image, it seems to be constituted from a small selection of facts which may be true of him, which facts are inflated into a dramatic and newsworthy appearance, and then used as a full picture of him. In consequence a special type of stigmatization can occur. The figure the individual cuts in daily life before those with whom he has routine dealings is likely to be dwarfed and spoiled by virtual demands (whether favorable or unfavorable) created by his public image. This seems especially to occur when the individual is no longer engaged in newsworthy larger events and must everywhere face being received as someone who no longer is what he once was; it seems also likely to occur when notoriety is acquired due to a brief and uncharacteristic, accidental event which exposes the individual to public identification without providing him any compensating claim to desired attributes.[45]

An implication of these comments is that the famous and the infamous may have more in common than either has with what headwaiters and gossip columnists call "nobodies," for whether a crowd wants to show love or hate for an individual, the same disruption of his ordinary movements can occur. (This type of lack of anonymity is to be contrasted to the type based on social

---

[45] In law, efforts of an individual to remain a private citizen or regain that status have come to form part of the question of privacy. A useful review may be found in M. Ernst and A. Schwartz, *Privacy: The Right to Be Let Alone* (New York: The Macmillan Company, 1962).

identity, as when an individual with a physical deformity feels he is being constantly stared at.) Infamous hangmen and famous actors have both found it expedient to board a train at an unanticipated station or to wear a disguise;[46] individuals may even find themselves using stratagems to escape hostile public attention that they also used at an earlier time in their story to escape adulatory attention. In any case, readily accessible information about the management of personal identity is to be found in the biographies and autobiographies of famous and infamous people.

An individual, then, may be seen as the central point in a distribution of persons who either merely know about him or know him personally, all of whom may have somewhat different amounts of information concerning him. Let me repeat that although the individual's daily round will routinely bring him into contact with individuals who know him differently, these differences will ordinarily not be incompatible; in fact, some kind of single biographical structure will be sustained. A man's relationship to his boss and his relationship to his child may be vastly different, so that he cannot easily play the part of employee while playing the part of father, but should the man, while walking with his child, meet his boss, a greeting and introduction will be possible without either the child or the boss radically reorganizing their personal identification of the man—both having known of the existence and role of the other. The well-established etiquette of the "courtesy introduction," in fact, assumes that the person we have a role relation to quite properly has other kinds of relationships to other kinds of persons. I assume, then, that the apparently haphazard contacts of everyday life may still constitute some kind of structure holding the individual to one biography, and this in spite of the multiplicity of selves that role and audience segregation allow him.

[46] See J. Atholl, *op. cit.*, Chap. 5, "The Public and the Press." On the famed avoiding contacts, see J. Bainbridge, *Garbo* (New York: Dell, 1961), especially pp. 205-206. On a current technique—the use of disguising wigs by movie stars who have their own hair—see L. Lieber, "Hollywood's Going Wig Wacky," *This Week*, Feb. 18, 1962.

Passing

It is apparent that if a stigmatizing affliction possessed by an individual is known to no one, including himself, as in the case, say, of someone with undiagnosed leprosy or unrecognized *petit mal* seizures, then the sociologist has no interest in it, except as a control device for learning about the "primary" [47] or objective implications of the stigma. Where the stigma is nicely invisible and known only to the person who possesses it, who tells no one, then here again is a matter of minor concern in the study of passing. The extent to which either of these two possibilities exists is of course hard to assess.

In a similar way, it should be clear that if a stigma were always immediately apparent to any and all persons with whom an individual had contact, then one's interest would be limited, too, although there would be some interest in the question of how much an individual can cut himself off from contact and still be allowed to function freely in society, in the question of tact and its breakdown, and in the question of self-derogation.

It is apparent, however, that these two extremes, where no one knows about the stigma and where everyone knows, fail to cover a great range of cases. First, there are important stigmas, such as the ones that prostitutes, thieves, homosexuals, beggars, and drug addicts have, which require the individual to be carefully secret about his failing to one class of persons, the police, while systematically exposing himself to other classes of persons, namely, clients, fellow-members, connections, fences, and the like.[48] Thus, no matter what role tramps assume in the presence of the police, they often have to declare themselves to housewives in order to obtain a free meal, and may even have to expose their status to passers-by because of being served on back porches what they understandably call "exhibition meals." [49] Secondly, even where an individual could keep an unapparent

---

[47] In the sense introduced by Lemert, *Social Pathology, op. cit.*, pp. 75 ff.
[48] See T. Hirshi, "The Professional Prostitute," *Berkeley Journal of Sociology*, VII (1962), 36.
[49] E. Kane, "The Jargon of the Underworld," *Dialect Notes*, V (1927), 445.

stigma secret, he will find that intimate relations with others, ratified in our society by mutual confession of invisible failings, cause him either to admit his situation to the intimate or to feel guilty for not doing so. In any case, nearly all matters which are very secret are still known to someone, and hence cast a shadow.

Similarly, there are many cases where it appears that an individual's stigma will always be apparent, but where this proves to be not quite the case; for on examination one finds that the individual will occasionally be in a position to elect to conceal crucial information about himself. For example, while a lame boy may seem always to present himself as such, strangers can momentarily assume that he has been in a temporarily incapacitating accident,[50] just as a blind person led into a dark cab by a friend may find for a moment that sight has been imputed to her,[51] or a blind man wearing dark glasses sitting in a dark bar may be taken as a seeing person by a newcomer,[52] or a double hand-amputee with hooks watching a movie may cause a sexually forward female sitting next to him to scream in terror over what her hand has suddenly found.[53] Similarly, black skinned Negroes who have never passed publicly may nonetheless find themselves, in writing letters or making telephone calls, projecting an image of self that is subject to later discrediting.

Given these several possibilities that fall between the extremes of complete secrecy on one hand and complete information on the other, it would seem that the problems people face who make a concerted and well-organized effort to pass are problems that wide ranges of persons face at some time or other. Because of the great rewards in being considered normal, almost all persons who are in a position to pass will do so on some occasion by intent. Further, the individual's stigma may relate to matters which cannot be appropriately divulged to strangers. An ex-convict, for example, can only disclose his stigma widely by im-

[50] F. Davis, "Polio in the Family: A Study in Crisis and Family Process," Ph.D. Dissertation, University of Chicago, 1958, p. 236.
[51] Davis, "Deviance Disavowal," *op. cit.*, p. 124.
[52] S. Rigman, *Second Sight* (New York: David McKay, 1959), p. 101.
[53] Russell, *op. cit.*, p. 124.

properly presuming on mere acquaintances, orally disclosing to them personal facts about himself which are more personal than the relationship really warrants. A conflict between candor and seemliness will often be resolved in favor of the latter. Finally, when the stigma relates to parts of the body that the normally qualified must themselves conceal in public places, then passing is inevitable, whether desired or not. A woman who has had a mastectomy or a Norwegian male sex offender who has been penalized by castration are forced to present themselves falsely in almost all situations, having to conceal their unconventional secrets because of everyone's having to conceal the conventional ones.

When an individual in effect or by intent passes, it is possible for a discrediting to occur because of what becomes apparent about him, apparent even to those who socially identify him solely on the basis of what is available to any stranger in the social situation. (Thus arises one variety of what is called "an embarrassing incident.") But this kind of threat to virtual social identity is certainly not the only kind. Apart from the fact that the individual's current actions can discredit his current pretensions, a basic contingency in passing is that he will be discovered by those who can personally identify him and who include in their biographical record of him unapparent facts that are incompatible with present claims. It is then, incidentally, that personal identification bears strongly on social identity.

Here, of course, is the basis of the varieties of blackmail. There is the "frame-up," this consisting of the engineering of a happening now that can be used as a basis of blackmail shortly. (A frame-up is to be distinguished from "entrapment," an art detectives practice to cause criminals to reveal their habitual criminal practices and thus their criminal identity.) There is "pre-blackmail," where the victim is forced to continue in a course of action because of the blackmailer's warning that any change will lead him to disclose facts making the change untenable. W. I. Thomas cites an actual case in which a policeman forces a prostitute to remain in her lucrative calling by systematically discrediting her attempts to obtain employment as a well-reputed girl.[54] There is "self-saving blackmail," perhaps the most important kind, where the blackmailer, by intent or in effect, avoids paying an earned penalty because enforcing payment would result in the creditor's discrediting.

> The "presumption of innocence until guilt is proven" provides far less protection for the unwed mother than for the unmarried father. Her guilt is made obvious by a protruding profile—evidence hard to conceal. He bears no outward signs, and his accessory role must be proved. But to provide such a proof, when the state does not assume the initiative in establishing paternity, the unwed mother must disclose her identity and sexual misbehavior to a larger audience. Her reluctance to do this makes it fairly easy for her male accomplice to maintain his anonymity and his ostensible innocence, if he chooses.[55]

Finally, there is "full" or classic blackmail, the blackmailer obtaining payments by threatening to disclose facts about the individual's past or present which could utterly discredit his currently sustained identity. It may be noted that all full blackmail includes the self-saving kind, since the successful blackmailer, in addition to obtaining the blackmail, also avoids the penalty attached to blackmailing.

Sociologically, blackmail itself may not be very important;[56] it is more important to consider the kinds of relations an individual can have to those who could, if they wanted to, blackmail him. It is here that one sees that a person who passes leads a double life, and that the informational connectedness of biography can allow for different modes of double living.

[54] *The Unadjusted Girl* (Boston: Little, Brown & Company, 1923), pp. 144-145.
[55] E. Clark, *Unmarried Mothers* (New York: Free Press of Glencoe, 1961), p. 4.
[56] Given the profusion of skeletons in people's closets, it is a wonder that full blackmail is not more prevalent. The legal sanction is of course high, making the practice uncompetitive in many cases, but one still has to explain why the legal sanction is so high. Perhaps the rarity of the act and the strong sanction against it are both expressions of the distaste we have for work requiring us to confront unwilling others with greatly discrediting facts about themselves, this knowledge to be then pressed against their interests.

When the discreditable fact about an individual is in the past, he will be concerned not so much about original sources of evidence and information as about persons who can relay what they have already gathered. When the discreditable fact is part of current life, then he must guard against more than relayed information; he must guard against getting directly caught in the act, as a call girl suggests:

> Exposure was possible without arrest, and equally painful. "I always look around a room fast when I go to parties," she said. "You never know. Once I ran smack into two of my cousins. They were with a couple of call girls and didn't even nod to me. I took my cue—hoping they were too busy thinking of themselves to wonder about me. I always wondered what I would do if I ran into my father, since he was around quite a bit." [57]

If there is something discreditable about an individual's past or present, it would seem that the precariousness of his position will vary directly with the number of persons who are in on the secret; the more who know about his shady side the more treacherous his situation. Hence it may be safer for a bank teller to dally with his wife's girlfriend than to go to the races

Whether those in the know are many or few, there is here a simple double life containing those who think they know the whole man and those who "really" do so. This possibility must be contrasted to the situation of the individual who lives a double double life, moving in two circles each of which is unaware that the other exists with its own and different biography of him. A man carrying on an affair, with perhaps a small number of individuals knowing that this is so and even associating with the illicit couple, is carrying on a single double life. However, should the illicit couple begin to make friends who are unaware that the couple are really not a couple, a double double life begins to emerge. The danger in the first type of double living is that of blackmail or malicious disclosure; the

---

[57] Stearn, *Sisters of the Night*, op. cit., pp. 96-97.

danger in the second type, the greater, perhaps, is that of inadvertent disclosure, since none of those who knows the couple will be oriented to maintaining the secret, being unaware that there is one to keep.

I have considered so far a currently sustained life that is threatened by what some others know about the individual's past or about the shady parts of his present. Now another perspective on double living must be considered.

When an individual leaves a community after residing there for some years, he leaves a personal identification behind, often with a well-rounded biography attached, including assumptions as to how he is likely to "end up." In his current community the individual will develop a biography in others' minds too, potentially a full portrait including a version of the kind of person he used to be and the background out of which he came. Obviously, a discrepancy may arise between these two sets of knowings about him; something like a double biography can develop, with those who knew him when and those who know him now each thinking that they know the whole man.

Often this biographical discontinuity is bridged by his affording accurate and adequate information about his past to those in his present, and by those in his past bringing their biographies of him up to date through news and gossip about him. This bridging is eased when what he has become is not a discredit upon what he was, and when what he was does not discredit too much what he has become, which of course is the usual state of affairs. In brief, there will be discontinuities in his biography but not discrediting ones.

Now while students are sufficiently alive to the effect on the individual's present of having had a blameworthy past, insufficient attention has been given to the effect upon his earlier biographers of a blameworthy present. There has been insufficient appreciation of the importance to an individual of preserving a good memory of himself among those with whom he no longer lives, even though this fact fits nicely into what is called reference group theory. The classic case here is that of the prostitute who, although adjusted to her urban round and the contacts she routinely has in it, fears to "bump into" a man from her home town who will of course be able to discern her present social attributes and bring the news back home.[58] In this case her closet is as big as her beat, and she is the skeleton that resides in it. This sentimental concern with those with whom we no longer have actual dealings provides one of the penalties of taking on an immoral occupation, illustrated in Park's comment that it is bums, not bankers, who decline to have their pictures in the paper, a modesty due to fear of being recognized by someone from home.

In the literature there is some suggestion of a natural cycle of passing.[59] The cycle may start with unwitting passing that the passer never learns he is engaging in; move from there to unintended passing that the surprised passer learns about in mid-passage; from there to passing "for fun"; passing during non-routine parts of the social round, such as vacations and travel; passing during routine daily occasions, such as at work or in service establishments; finally, "disappearance"—complete passing over in all areas of life, the secret being known only to the passer himself. It may be noted that when relatively complete passing is essayed, the individual sometimes consciously arranges his own *rite de passage*, going to another city, holing up in a room for a few days with preselected clothing and cosmetics he has brought with him, and then, like a butterfly, emerging

[58] See, for example, *Street-Walker* (New York: Dell, 1961), pp. 194-196. Although there is ample fictional, and even some case-history, material on prostitutes, there is very little material of any kind on pimps. (But see, for example, C. MacInnes, *Mr. Love and Justice* [London: The New English Library, 1962]; and J. Murtagh and S. Harris, *Cast the First Stone* [New York: Pocket Books, 1958], Chaps. 8 and 9.) This is a great pity, since there is perhaps no male occupation about which its performers are more bashful. The daily round of the pimp must be full of passing dodges not yet recorded. Further, only with the greatest difficulty can pimps be tactfully told to their faces what their occupation is. Here is a good opportunity, then, to gather material on the situation of the discredited as well as the discreditable.

[59] See H. Cayton and S. Drake, *Black Metropolis* (London: Jonathan Cape, 1946), "A Rose by Any Other Name," pp. 159-171. I am indebted here to an unpublished paper by Gary Marx.

to try the brand new wings.[60] At any phase, of course, there can be a break in the cycle and a return to the fold.

If it is not possible at this time to speak of such a cycle with any assurance, and if it is necessary to suggest that some discreditable attributes preclude the final phases of the cycle, it is at least possible to look for various points of stability in passing penetration; certainly it is possible to see that the extent of passing can vary, from momentary and unintended at one extreme to the classic kind of deliberate total passing.

Earlier, two phases in the learning process of the stigmatized person were suggested: his learning the normal point of view and learning that he is disqualified according to it. Presumably a next phase consists of his learning to cope with the way others treat the kind of person he can be shown to be. A still later phase is now my concern, namely, learning to pass.

Where a differentness is relatively unapparent, the individual must learn that in fact he can trust himself to secrecy. The point of view of observers of himself must be entered carefully, but not anxiously carried further than the observers themselves do. Starting with a feeling that everything known to himself is known to others, he often develops a realistic appreciation that this is not so. For example, it is reported that marihuana smokers slowly learn that when "high" they can function in the immediate presence of those who know them well, without these others discovering anything—a learning that apparently helps to transform an occasional user into a regular one.[61] Similarly, there are records of girls who, having just lost their virginity, examine themselves in the mirror to see if their stigma shows, only slowly coming to believe that in fact they look no different from the way they used to.[62] A parallel can be cited regarding the experience of a male after his first overt homosexual experience:

---

[60] See, for the passage from Negro to white, R. Lee, *I Passed for White* (New York: David McKay, 1955), pp. 89-92; from white to Negro, J. H. Griffin, *Black Like Me* (Boston: Houghton Mifflin, 1960), pp. 6-13.

[61] H. Becker, "Marihuana Use and Social Control," *Social Problems*, III (1955), 40.

[62] H. M. Hughes, ed., *The Fantastic Lodge* (Boston: Houghton Mifflin, 1961), p. 40.

INFORMATION CONTROL AND PERSONAL IDENTITY

> "Did it [his first homosexual experience] bother you later?" I asked.
>
> "Oh no, I only worried about somebody finding out. I was afraid my mother and dad could tell by looking at me. But they acted like always, and I began to feel confident and secure once more." [63]

It may be suggested that, due to social identity, the individual with a secret differentness will find himself during the daily and weekly round in three possible kinds of places. There will be forbidden or out-of-bounds places, where persons of the kind he can be shown to be are forbidden to be, and where exposure means expulsion—an eventuality often so unpleasant to all parties that a tacit cooperation will sometimes forestall it, the interloper providing a thin disguise and the rightfully present accepting it, even though both know the other knows of the interloping. There are civil places, where persons of the individual's kind, when known to be of his kind, are carefully, and sometimes painfully, treated as if they were not disqualified for routine acceptance, when in fact they somewhat are. Finally, there are back places, where persons of the individual's kind stand exposed and find they need not try to conceal their stigma, nor be overly concerned with cooperatively trying to disattend it. In some cases this license arises from having chosen the company of those with the same or a similar stigma. For example, it is said that carnivals provide physically handicapped employees with a world in which their stigma is relatively little an issue.[64] In other cases, the back place may be involuntarily created as a result of individuals being herded together administratively against their will on the basis of a common stigma. It might be added that whether the individual enters a back place voluntarily or involuntarily, the place is likely to provide an atmosphere of special piquancy. Here the individual will be able to be at ease among his fellows and also discover that acquaintances he thought were

[63] Stearn, *The Sixth Man, op. cit.*, p. 150.
[64] H. Viscardi, Jr., *A Laughter in the Lonely Night* (New York: Paul S. Eriksson, Inc., 1961), p. 309.

not of his own kind really are. However, as the following citation suggests, he will also run the risk of being easily discredited should a normal person known from elsewhere enter the place.

> A 17-year-old Mexican-American boy was committed to the hospital [for the mentally retarded] by the courts as a mental defective. He strongly rejected this definition, claiming that there was nothing wrong with him and that he wanted to go to a more "respectable" detention center for juvenile delinquents. Sunday morning, a few days after he arrived at the hospital, he was being taken to church with several other patients. By an unfortunate circumstance, his girl friend was visiting the hospital that morning with a friend whose infant brother was a patient at the hospital, and was walking toward him. When he saw her she had not yet seen him and he did not intend for her to do so. He turned from her and fled as fast as he could run, until overtaken by employees who thought he had gone berserk. When questioned about this behavior he explained that his girl friend did not know he was "in this place for dummies" and he could not bear the humiliation of being seen in the hospital as a patient.[65]

The beat of a prostitute constitutes for her the same kind of threat:

> It was this aspect of this social situation that I experienced when I visited the carriage roads in Hyde Park [a female social researcher states]. The deserted appearance of the footpaths and the apparent purposefulness of any woman who did walk along them were not only sufficient to announce my purpose to the public, they also forced upon me the realization that this area was reserved for prostitutes—it was a place set aside for them and would lend its colouring to anyone who chose to enter it—. . .[66]

This partitioning of the individual's world into forbidden, civil, and back places establishes the going price for revealing or concealing and the significance of being known about or not known about, whatever his choice of information strategies.

Just as the individual's world is divided up spatially by his

[65] Edgerton and Sabagh, *op. cit.*, p. 267.
[66] Rolph, *Women of the Streets, op. cit.*, pp. 56-57.

social identity, so also is it divided up by his personal identity. There are places where, as is said, he is known personally: either some of those present are likely to know him personally or the individual in charge of the area (hostess, maitre de, bartender, and the like) knows him personally, in either case assuring that his having been present there will be demonstrable later. Secondly, there are places where he can expect with some confidence not to "bump into" anyone who knows him personally, and where (barring the special contingencies faced by the famed and ill-famed, whom many persons know of without knowing personally) he can expect to remain anonymous, eventful to no one. Whether or not it is embarrassing to his personal identity to be in a place where, incidentally, he is known personally will vary of course with the circumstances, especially with the question of whom he is "with."

Given that the individual's spatial world will be divided into different regions according to the contingencies embedded in them for the management of social and personal identity, one can go on to consider some of the problems and consequences of passing. This consideration will partly overlap with folk wisdom; cautionary tales concerning the contingencies of passing form part of the morality we employ to keep people in their places.

He who passes finds unanticipated needs to disclose discrediting information about himself, as when a wife of a mental patient tries to collect her husband's unemployment insurance or a "married" homosexual tries to insure his house and finds he must try to explain his peculiar choice of beneficiary.[67] He also suffers from "in-deeper-ism," that is, pressure to elaborate a lie further and further to prevent a given disclosure.[68] His adaptive techniques can themselves give rise to hurt feelings and misunderstandings on the part of others.[69] His effort to conceal incapaci-

[67] Suggested by Evelyn Hooker in conversation.
[68] In regard to concealing mental hospital commitment of spouse, see Yarrow, Clausen, and Robbins, *op. cit.*, p. 42.
[69] On the deaf being inadvertently gauche and snobbish, see R. G. Barker *et al.*, *Adjustment to Physical Handicap and Illness* (New York: Social Science Research Council Bulletin No. 55, revised, 1953), pp. 193-194.

ties may cause him to display other ones or give the appearance of doing so: slovenliness, as when a near-blind person, affecting to see, trips over a stool, or spills drink down his shirt; inattentiveness, stubbornness, woodenness, or distance, as when a hard of hearing person fails to respond to a remark proffered him by someone ignorant of his shortcoming; sleepiness, as when a teacher perceives a student's *petit mal* epilepsy seizure as momentary daydreaming;[70] drunkenness, as when a man with cerebral palsy finds that his gait is always being misinterpreted.[71] Further, he who passes leaves himself open to learning what others "really" think of persons of his kind, both when they do not know they are dealing with someone of his kind and when they start out not knowing but learn part way through the encounter and sharply veer to another course. He finds himself not knowing how far information about himself has gone, this being a problem whenever his boss or schoolteacher is dutifully informed of his stigma, but others are not. As suggested, he can become subject to blackmail of various kinds by persons who know of his secret and do not have good reason for keeping quiet about it.

He who passes can also suffer the classic and central experience of exposure during face-to-face interaction, betrayed by the very weakness he is trying to hide, by the others present, or by impersonal circumstances. The situation of the stutterer is an example:

> We who stutter speak only when we must. We hide our defect, often so successfully that our intimates are surprised when in an unguarded moment, a word suddenly runs away with our tongues and we blurt and blat and grimace and choke until finally the spasm is over and we open our eyes to view the wreckage.[72]

---

[70] S. Livingston, *Living With Epileptic Seizures* (Springfield: Charles C Thomas, 1963), p. 32.
[71] Henrich and Kriegel, *op. cit.*, p. 101; see also p. 157.
[72] C. van Riper, *Do You Stutter?* (New York: Harper & Row, 1939), p. 601, in von Hentig, *op. cit.*, p. 100.

INFORMATION CONTROL AND PERSONAL IDENTITY

The epileptic subject to *grand mal* seizures provides a more extreme case; he may regain consciousness to find that he has been lying on a public street, incontinent, moaning, and jerking convulsively—a discrediting of sanity that is eased only slightly by his not being conscious during some of the episode.[73] I might add that the lore of every stigmatized grouping seems to have its own battery of cautionary tales of embarrassing exposure, and that most members seem able to provide examples from their own experiences.

Finally, he who passes can find himself called to a showdown by persons who have now learned of his secret and are about to confront him with his having been false. This possibility can even be formally instituted, as in mental health hearings and the following:

> Doreen, a Mayfair girl, says that court appearances are "about the worst part of it [i.e., prostitution]. You go in through that door and everyone's waiting for you and looking at you. I keep my head down and never look on either side. Then they say those awful words: 'Being a common prostitute . . .' and you feel awful, all the time not knowing who's watching you at the back of the court. You say 'guilty' and get out as soon as you can." [74]

The presence of fellow-sufferers (or the wise) introduces a special set of contingencies in regard to passing, since the very techniques used to conceal stigmas may give the show away to someone who is familiar with the tricks of the trade, the assumption being that it takes one (or those close to him) to know one:

> "Why don't you try a chiropractor?" she [a casual acquaintance] asked me, chewing corned beef, giving no slightest indication that she was about to knock the bottom out of my world. "Dr. Fletcher told me he's curing one of his patients of deafness."
> My heart skittered, in panic, against my ribs. What did she mean?

---

[73] Livingston, *op. cit.*, pp. 30 ff.
[74] Rolph, *Women of the Streets, op. cit.*, p. 24. For a general statement, see H. Garfinkel, "Conditions of Successful Degradation Ceremonies," *American Journal of Sociology*, LXI (1956), 420-424.

"My dad's deaf," she revealed. "I can spot a deaf person anywhere. That soft voice of yours. And that trick of letting your sentences trail off—not finishing them. Dad does that all the time."[75]

These contingencies help to explain the ambivalence previously mentioned that the individual may feel when confronted with his own kind. As Wright suggests:

> ... a person who wishes to conceal his disability will notice disability-revealing mannerisms in another person. Moreover, he is likely to resent those mannerisms that advertise the fact of disability, for in wishing to conceal his disability he wishes others to conceal theirs. Thus it is that the person who is hard of hearing and who strives to hide this fact will be annoyed at the old woman who cups her hand behind her ear. Flaunting disability is a threat to him because it stirs up the guilt of having scorned his own group membership as well as the possibility of his own exposure. He may prefer surreptitiously to realize the other person's secret and to maintain a gentlemen's agreement that both should play their "as if" roles to having the other person challenge his pretense by confiding his own.[76]

Control of identity information has a special bearing on relationships. Relationships can necessitate time spent together, and the more time the individual spends with another the more chance the other will acquire discrediting information about him. Further, as already suggested, every relationship obliges the related persons to exchange an appropriate amount of intimate facts about self, as evidence of trust and mutual commitment. Close relationships that the individual had before he came to have something to conceal therefore become compromised, automatically deficient in shared information. Newly formed or "post-stigma" relationships are very likely to carry the discreditable person past the point where he feels it has been honorable of him to withhold the facts. And, in some cases, even very fleeting relationships can constitute a danger, since the

---
[75] F. Warfield, *Cotton in My Ears* (New York: The Viking Press, 1948), p. 44, in Wright, *op. cit.*, p. 215.
[76] Wright, *op. cit.*, p. 41.

small talk suitable between strangers who have struck up a conversation can touch on secret failings, as when the wife of an impotent husband must answer questions as to how many children she has and, having none, why so.[77]

The phenomenon of passing has always raised issues regarding the psychic state of the passer. First, it is assumed that he must necessarily pay a great psychological price, a very high level of anxiety, in living a life that can be collapsed at any moment. A statement by a wife of a mental patient will illustrate:

> ... and suppose after George gets out everything is going well and somebody throws it up in his face. That would ruin everything. I live in terror of that—a complete terror of that.[78]

I think that close study of passers would show that this anxiety is not always found and that here our folk conceptions of human nature can be seriously misleading.

Secondly, it is often assumed, and with evidence, that the passer will feel torn between two attachments. He will feel some alienation from his new "group," for he is unlikely to be able to identify fully with their attitude to what he knows he can be shown to be.[79] And presumably he will suffer feelings of disloyalty and self-contempt when he cannot take action against "offensive" remarks made by members of the category he is passing into against the category he is passing out of—especially when he himself finds it dangerous to refrain from joining in this vilification. As discreditable persons suggest:

> When jokes were made about "queers" I had to laugh with the rest, and when talk was about women I had to invent conquests of my own. I hated myself at such moments, but there seemed to be nothing else that I could do. My whole life became a lie.[80]

[77] "Vera Vaughan," in Toynbee, *op. cit.*, p. 126.
[78] Yarrow, Clausen, and Robbins, *op. cit.*, p. 34.
[79] Riesman, *op. cit.*, p. 114.
[80] Wildeblood, *op. cit.*, p. 32.

> The tone of voice sometimes used [by friends] to refer to spinsters would shock me, as I felt I was cheating by in fact being in the state which married people looked at askance, while having the apparent status of a married woman. I also felt somewhat dishonest with my unmarried woman friends who did not talk about these matters but eyed me with some curiosity and envy for having an experience which I did not in fact enjoy.[81]

Thirdly, it seems to be assumed, and apparently correctly, that he who passes will have to be alive to aspects of the social situation which others treat as uncalculated and unattended. What are unthinking routines for normals can become management problems for the discreditable.[82] These problems cannot always be handled by past experience, since new contingencies always arise, making former concealing devices inadequate. The person with a secret failing, then, must be alive to the social situation as a scanner of possibilities, and is therefore likely to be alienated from the simpler world in which those around him apparently dwell. What is their ground is his figure. A young man who is near blind provides one example:

> I managed to keep Mary from knowing my eyes were bad through two dozen sodas and three movies. I used every trick I had ever learned. I paid special attention to the color of her dress each morning, and then I would keep my eyes and ears and my sixth sense alert for anyone that might be Mary. I didn't take any chances. If I wasn't sure, I would greet whoever it was with familiarity. They probably thought I was nuts, but I didn't care. I always held her hand on the way to and from the movies at night, and she led me, without knowing it, so I didn't have to feel for curbs and steps.[83]

A young boy with a "stricture," who cannot pass water when in the presence of others, wanting to keep his differentness a secret, finds himself having to plot and plan and be wary, where others are merely having to be boys:

---

[81] "Vera Vaughan," in Toynbee, *op. cit.*, p. 122.
[82] Here, again, I am indebted to Harold Garfinkel.
[83] Criddle, *op. cit.*, p. 79.

When I went away to boarding school at the age of ten there were new difficulties, and new ways of dealing with them had to be found. Generally speaking, it was never a case of making water when one wanted to, but always a case of doing so when one could. I felt it necessary to keep my disability secret from the other boys, since the worst thing that can happen to a boy at his prep. school is to be in any way "different"; so I went when they did to the school latrines, though nothing happened there but the increase of my envy of my fellows' freedom to behave naturally, and even challenge one another to see how high up the wall they could reach. (I should have liked to join in, but if anyone challenged me, I had always "just finished.") I used various stratagems. One was to ask to be excused during class, when the latrines would be deserted. Another was to stay awake at night and use the pot under my bed when the dormitory's other occupants were asleep, or at least when it was dark and I could not be seen.[84]

Similarly, one learns of the constant wariness of stutterers:

We have many ingenious tricks for disguising or minimizing our blocks. We look ahead for "Jonah" sounds and words, so-called because they are unlucky and we envy the whale his ease in expelling them. We dodge "Jonah" words when we can, substituting non-feared words in their places or hastily shifting our thought until the continuity of our speech becomes as involved as a plate of spaghetti.[85]

And about the wife of a mental patient:

Concealment often becomes cumbersome. Thus, to keep the neighbors from knowing the husband's hospital (having reported that he was in a hospital because of suspicion of cancer), Mrs. G. must rush to her apartment to get the mail before her neighbors pick it up for her as they used to do. She has had to abandon second breakfasts at the drugstore with the women in the neighboring apartments to avoid their questions. Before she can allow visitors in her apartment, she must pick up any material identifying the hospital, and so on.[86]

---

[84] "N. O. Goe," in Toynbee, *op. cit.*, p. 150.
[85] Riper, *op. cit.*, p. 601, in von Hentig, *op. cit.*, p. 100.
[86] Yarrow, Clausen, and Robbins, *op. cit.*, p. 42.

And from a homosexual:

> The strain of deceiving my family and friends often became intolerable. It was necessary for me to watch every word I spoke, and every gesture that I made, in case I gave myself away.[87]

A similar scanning may be illustrated among colostomy patients:

> "I never go to local movies. If I do go to the movie I select a large house like Radio City where I have greater choice of seats and can pick an end seat where I can rush to the bathroom if I have gas."[88]

> "When I go on a bus I pick my seat just in case. I sit on an end seat or near the door."[89]

In all of this, special timing may be required. Thus, there is the practice of "living on a leash"—the Cinderella syndrome—whereby the discreditable person stays close to the place where he can refurbish his disguise, and where he can rest up from having to wear it; he moves from his repair station only that distance that he can return from without losing control over information about himself:

> Since irrigation does constitute the primary defense against the occurrence of spillage, as well as representing a reparative activity of great emotional significance, patients with a colostomy frequently schedule travel and social contacts in relation to the time and effectiveness of irrigation. Travel is usually restricted to the distance which can be traversed in the interval between irrigations at home, and social contacts are limited to periods between irrigation which are believed to afford maximum protection against spillage or flatus. Patients can, therefore, be considered as living "on a leash" which is only as long as the time interval between irrigations.[90]

There is a final issue to be considered. As already suggested, a child with a stigma can pass in a special way. Parents, knowing

---
[87] Wildeblood, *op. cit.*, p. 32.
[88] Orbach *et al.*, *op. cit.*, p. 164.
[89] *Ibid.*
[90] Orbach *et al.*, *op. cit.*, p. 159.

of their child's stigmatic condition, may encapsulate him with domestic acceptance and ignorance of what he is going to have to become. When he ventures outdoors he does so therefore as an unwitting passer, at least to the extent that his stigma is not immediately apparent. At this point his parents are faced with a basic dilemma regarding information management, sometimes appealing to medical practitioners for strategies.[91] If the child is informed about himself at school age, it is felt he may not be strong enough psychologically to bear the news, and in addition may tactlessly disclose these facts about himself to those who need not know. On the other hand, if he is kept too long in the dark, then he will not be prepared for what is to happen to him and, moreover, may be informed about his condition by strangers who have no reason to take the time and care required to present the facts in a constructive, hopeful light.

Techniques of Information Control

It has been suggested that an individual's social identity divides up the world of people and places for him, and that his personal identity does this too, although differently. It is these frames of reference one must apply in studying the daily round of a particular stigmatized person, as he wends his way to and from his place of work, his place of residence, his place of shopping, and the places where he participates in recreation. A key concept here is the daily round, for it is the daily round that links the individual to his several social situations. And one studies the daily round with a special perspective in mind. To the extent that the individual is a discredited person, one looks for the routine cycle of restrictions he faces regarding social acceptance; to the extent that he is discreditable, for the contingencies he faces in managing information about himself. For example, an individual with a facial deformity can expect, as suggested, to cease gradually to be a shocking surprise to those in his own

[91] For a practitioner's version of childhood epilepsy as a problem in information control, see Livingston, *op. cit.*, "Should Epilepsy Be Publicized," pp 201-210

neighborhood, and there he can obtain a small measure of acceptance; at the same time, articles of dress worn to conceal part of his deformity will have less effect here than they will in parts of the city where he is unknown and otherwise treated less well.

Some of the common techniques the individual with a secret defect employs in managing crucial information about himself can now be considered.

Obviously, one strategy is to conceal or obliterate signs that have come to be stigma symbols. Name-changing is a well-known example.[92] Drug addicts provide another example:

> [Re a New Orleans anti-drug drive:] The cops began stopping addicts on the street and examining their arms for needle marks. If they found marks, they pressured the addict to sign a statement admitting his condition so he could be charged under the "drug addicts law." The addicts were promised a suspended sentence if they would plead guilty and get the new law started. Addicts ransacked their persons looking for veins to shoot in outside the arm area. If the law could find no marks on a man they usually let him go. If they found marks they would hold him for seventy-two hours and try to make him sign a statement.[93]

It should be noted that since the physical equipment employed to mitigate the "primary" impairment of some handicaps understandably becomes a stigma symbol, there will be a desire to reject using it. An example is the individual with declining eye sight who avoids wearing bifocal glasses because these might suggest old age. But of course this strategy can interfere with compensatory measures. Hence the making of this corrective equipment invisible will have a double function. The hard of hearing provide an illustration of the using of these unapparent correctives:

[92] See L. Broom, H. P. Beem, and V. Harris, "Characteristics of 1,107 Petitioners for Change of Name," *American Sociological Review*, XX (1955), 33-39.
[93] W. Lee, *Junkie* (New York: Ace Books, 1953), p. 91.

INFORMATION CONTROL AND PERSONAL IDENTITY

> Aunt Mary [a hard of hearing relative] knew all about early sound receptors, innumerable variations of the ear trumpet. She had pictures showing how such receptors had been built into hats, ornamental combs, canteens, walking sticks; hidden in arm chairs, in flower vases for the dining-room table; even hidden in men's beards.[94]

A more current illustration is "inviso-blended lenses"—bifocals which do not show a "dividing line."

The concealment of stigma symbols sometimes occurs along with a related process, the use of disidentifiers, as can be illustrated from the practices of James Berry, England's first fully professionalized hangman:

> It is doubtful whether violence on Berry was ever really planned, but his reception in the streets was such that he took good care whenever possible to avoid being recognized. He told one interviewer that on a number of occasions when travelling to Ireland he concealed his rope and straps about his person so that he was not given away by the Gladstone bag, which was almost as much a mark of his trade as the little black bag was of the Victorian doctor. His sense of isolation and being disliked by everyone he met probably explained the extraordinary episode when his wife and small son accompanied him to Ireland for an execution, although the explanation he offered was that it was to conceal his identity, since—he rightly guessed—no one would suppose that a man walking along holding the hand of a ten-year-old boy would be the executioner on his way to hang a murderer.[95]

One deals here with what espionage literature calls a "cover," and with what another literature describes as a conjugal service possible when a male homosexual and a female homosexual suppress their inclinations and marry one another.

When the individual's stigma is established in him during his stay in an institution, and when the institution retains a dis-

[94] Warfield, *Keep Listening, op. cit.*, p. 41.
[95] Atholl, *op. cit.*, pp. 88-89.

crediting hold upon him for a period after his release, one may expect a special cycle of passing. For example, in one mental hospital [96] it was found that patients re-entering the community often planned to pass in some degree. Patients who were forced to rely on the rehabilitation officer, the social service worker, or the employment agencies for a job, often discussed among their fellows the contingencies they faced and the standard strategy for dealing with them. For the first job, official entree would necessitate the employer knowing about their stigma, and perhaps the personnel officer, but always the lower levels of the organization and workmates could be kept in some ignorance. As suggested, it was felt that this could involve a certain amount of insecurity because it would not be known for sure who "knew" and who didn't, and how long-lasting would be the ignorance of those who didn't know. Patients expressed the feeling that after staying in a placement job of this kind for six months, long enough to save some money and get loose from hospital agencies, they would quit work and, on the basis of the six-month work record, get a job someplace else, this time trusting that everyone at work could be kept ignorant of the stay in a mental hospital.[97]

Another strategy of those who pass is to present the signs of their stigmatized failing as signs of another attribute, one that is less significantly a stigma. Mental defectives, for example, apparently sometimes try to pass as mental patients, the latter being the lesser of the two social evils.[98] Similarly, a hard of hearing person may intentionally style her conduct to give others the impression that she is a daydreamer, an absent-minded person, an indifferent, easily bored person—even someone who is feeling faint, or snores and therefore is unable to answer quiet questions since she is obviously asleep. These character traits

---

[96] See the writer's study of St. Elizabeths Hospital, Washington, D. C., partly reported in *Asylums* (New York: Doubleday & Co., Anchor Books, 1961).

[97] For evidence on the frequency of ex-patients employing such a passing cycle, see M. Linder and D. Landy, "Post-Discharge Experience and Vocational Rehabilitation Needs of Psychiatric Patients," *Mental Hygiene*, XLII (1958), 39.

[98] Edgerton and Sabagh, *op. cit.*, p. 268.

INFORMATION CONTROL AND PERSONAL IDENTITY 95

account for failure to hear without requiring the imputation of deafness.[99]

A very widely employed strategy of the discreditable person is to handle his risks by dividing the world into a large group to whom he tells nothing, and a small group to whom he tells all and upon whose help he then relies; he co-opts for his masquerade just those individuals who would ordinarily constitute the greatest danger. In the case of close relationships he already has at the time of acquiring the stigma he may immediately "bring the relationship up to date," by means of a quiet confidential talk; thereafter he may be rejected, but he retains his standing as someone who relates honorably. Interestingly, this kind of information management is often recommended by medical practitioners, especially when they have to be the first to inform the individual of his stigma. Thus, medical officials who discover a case of leprosy may suggest that the new secret be kept among the doctors, the patient, and his immediate family,[100] perhaps offering this discretion in order to ensure continued cooperation from the patient. In the case of post-stigma relationships that have gone past the point where the individual should have told, he can stage a confessional scene with as much emotional fuss as the unfairness of his past silence requires, and then throw himself on the other's mercy as someone doubly exposed, exposed first in his differentness and secondly in his dishonesty and untrustworthiness. There are fine records of these touching scenes,[101] and a need to understand the huge amount of forget-and-forgiveness they can call forth. No doubt a factor in the rate of success of these confessions is the tendency for the concealer to feel out the concealed-from to make sure before-

[99] Warfield, *Cotton in My Ears, op. cit.*, pp. 21, 29-30, in Wright, *op. cit.*, pp. 23-24. A general statement is provided by Lemert, *Social Pathology, op. cit.*, p. 95, under the heading, "counterfeit roles."

[100] B. Rouerché, "A Lonely Road," *Eleven Blue Men* (New York: Berkley Publishing Corp., 1953), p. 122.

[101] For a scene between a pregnant prostitute and the unknowing man who wants to marry her, see Thomas, *op. cit.*, p. 134; for a fictionalized scene between a passing Negro and the white girl he wants to marry, see Johnson, *op. cit.*, pp. 204-205.

hand that the revelation will be received without complete rupture of the relationship. Note that the stigmatized individual is almost foredoomed to these scenes; new relationships are often ones that can easily be discouraged before they take hold, making immediate honesty necessarily costly and hence often avoided.

As already implied, a person who is in a position to blackmail is also often in a position to help the blameworthy individual maintain his secret; moreover he is likely to have many motives for doing so. Thus, managers of resort establishments often enforce a privacy policy that protects the marital truants who sometimes stay or play in these places. Pimps are sometimes similarly solicitous:

> The men [pimps] rented rooms in respectable hotels, on the first floor above the lobby, so that their customers could use the stairways without being seen by elevator men or desk clerks.[102]

As are their colleagues:

> If their clients are prominent people the girls will not readily identify them or name them in conversation even with each other.[103]

Similarly one reads of the role of a hairdresser employed by girls in a "first-class" house of prostitution:

> Indeed, he was more than an artist; he was a sincere friend to every girl in the house, and "Charlie" heard confidences that were seldom given to others, and gave much common-sense advice. Moreover, in his own home on Michigan Avenue he received the mail of girls who were keeping their profession secret from families and friends, and his house served as a place where the girls could meet relatives who came unexpectedly to Chicago.[104]

Other illustrations are provided by marital pairs in which one member belongs to a stigmatized category and the other mem-

---
[102] Stearn, *Sisters of the Night, op. cit.*, p. 13.
[103] H. Greenwald, *The Call Girl* (New York: Ballantine Books, 1958), p. 24.
[104] *Madeleine, op. cit.*, p. 71.

INFORMATION CONTROL AND PERSONAL IDENTITY

ber carries a courtesy card. For example, it is suggested that the mate of an alcoholic will help the alcoholic in concealing his failing. The wife of a colostomy case will help him check to make sure that he doesn't smell,[105] and further, may be

> ... stationed in the house to intercept any phone calls or door bells so that irrigation can continue uninterruptedly. . . .[106]

The husband of a woman with only the appearance of normal hearing helped in the following manner:

> He himself was an awfully nice man, and from the moment we fell in love he knew instinctively how to help me cover my blank spots and redeem my mistakes. He had a clear, resonant voice. He never seemed to raise it, but I always heard what he said; at least, he let me think I did. When we were with other people he watched to see how I was doing and when I floundered he unobtrusively gave me clues to keep me afloat in the conversational stream.[107]

It should be added that intimates not only help the discreditable person in his masquerade but can also carry this function past the point of the beneficiary's knowledge; they can in fact serve as a protective circle, allowing him to think he is more fully accepted as a normal person than in fact is the case. They will therefore be more alive to his differentness and its problems than he will himself. Here, certainly, the notion that stigma management only concerns the stigmatized individual and strangers is inadequate.

Interestingly enough, those who share a particular stigma can often rely upon mutual aid in passing, again illustrating that those who can be most threatening are often those who can render most assistance. For example, when one homosexual accosts another, the action may be carried out in such a way that normals are unaware that anything out of the ordinary is occurring:

[105] Orbach *et al.*, *op. cit.*, p. 163.
[106] *Ibid.*, p. 153.
[107] Warfield, *Keep Listening*, *op. cit.*, p. 21.

If we watch very carefully, and know what to watch for in a "gay" bar, we begin to observe that some individuals are apparently communicating with each other without exchanging words, but simply by exchanging glances—but not the kind of quick glance which ordinarily occurs between men.[108]

The same kind of cooperativeness is to be found among the circles of stigmatized persons who know one another personally. For example, ex-mental patients who knew each other in the institution may maintain tactful control of this fact on the outside. In some cases, as when one of the individuals is with normals, the individual may give and be given the "go by," the passing by of each other as though they were unacquainted. Where a greeting does occur, it may be handled discreetly; the context of the initial acquaintanceship is not made explicit, and the individual whose situation is the more delicate is accorded the right to pace the acknowledgment and the sociable exchange that follows from it. Ex-mental patients are not alone here of course:

> The professional call girl has a code regulating her relations with the client. For example, it is customary for a call girl never to show any signs of recognizing a customer when she meets him in public, unless he greets her first.[109]

Where this kind of discretion is not afforded, one can sometimes expect the discredited individual to take active disciplinary action, as Reiss, in his paper on juvenile entrepreneurs, illustrates by quoting an informant.

> I was walkin' down the street with my steady girl when this gay drives by that I'd been with once before and he whistles at me and

---

[108] E. Hooker, "The Homosexual Community," unpublished paper read at the Fourteenth International Congress of Applied Psychology, Copenhagen, August 14, 1961, p. 8. The structure of such a meeting of glances is complex, involving mutual cognitive recognition of social (but not personal) identity; sexual intent is also involved, and sometimes a tacit contract.

[109] Greenwald, *op. cit.*, p. 24.

calls, "Hi, Sweetie." ... And, was I mad ... so I went down to where the boys was and we laid for him and beat on him 'til he like to a never come to ... ain't gonna take nothin' like that off'n a queer.[110]

It is to be expected that voluntary maintenance of various types of distance will be employed strategically by those who pass, the discreditable here using much the same devices as do the discredited, but for slightly different reasons. By declining or avoiding overtures of intimacy the individual can avoid the consequent obligation to divulge information. By keeping relationships distant he ensures that time will not have to be spent with the other, for, as already stated, the more time that is spent with another the more chance of unanticipated events that disclose secrets. Examples may be cited from the stigma management work done by wives of mental patients:

But I've cut off all our other friends [after citing five who "knew"]. I didn't tell them that I was giving up the apartment and I had the phone disconnected without telling anyone so they don't know how to get in touch with me.[111]

I haven't gotten too friendly with anyone at the office because I don't want people to know where my husband is. I figure that if I got too friendly with them, then they would start asking questions, and I might start talking, and I just think it's better if as few people as possible know about Joe.[112]

By maintaining physical distance, the individual can also restrict the tendency of others to build up a personal identification of him. By residing in a region with a mobile population, he can limit the amount of continuous experience others have of him. By residing in a region cut off from one he ordinarily frequents he can introduce a disconnectedness in his biography: whether

---

[110] A. J. Reiss, Jr., "The Social Integration of Queers and Peers," *Social Problems*, IX (1961), 118.
[111] Yarrow, Clausen, and Robbins, *op. cit.*, p. 36.
[112] *Ibid.*

intentionally, as in the case of an unmarried pregnant girl going out of state to have her child, or of small-town homosexuals going to New York, Los Angeles, or Paris for relatively anonymous activity; or unintentionally, as in the case of the mental patient who gratefully finds that his place of commitment is far out of town and hence somewhat cut off from his ordinary contacts. By staying indoors and not answering the phone or door, the discreditable individual can remove himself from most of those contacts in which his disgrace might be established as part of the biography others have of him.[113]

A final possibility must now be considered, one that allows the individual to forego all the others. He can voluntarily disclose himself, thereby radically transforming his situation from that of an individual with information to manage to that of an individual with uneasy social situations to manage, from that of a discreditable person to that of a discredited one. Once a secretly stigmatized person has given information about himself it becomes possible, of course, for him to engage in any of the adaptive actions previously cited as being available to the known-to-be stigmatized, this accounting in part for his policy of self-disclosure.

One method of disclosure is for the individual voluntarily to wear a stigma symbol, a highly visible sign that advertises his failing wherever he goes. There are, for example, hard of hearing persons who wear a batteryless hearing aid;[114] the partly blind who affect a collapsible white cane; Jewesses who wear a Star of David as a necklace. It should be noted that some of these stigma symbols, such as a Knights of Columbus lapel button indicating that the wearer is Catholic, are not frankly presented as disclosures of stigma, but purportedly attest rather to membership in organizations claimed to have no such significance in themselves. It should be noted also that militant programs of all kinds can be served by this device, for the self-symbolizing indi-

---

[113] An example regarding concealment of illegitimate pregnancy is given in H. M. Hughes, *op. cit.*, pp. 53 ff.
[114] Barker *et al.*, *Adjustment to Physical Handicap and Illness*, *op. cit.*, p. 241.

vidual ensures his being cut off from the society of normals. The manner in which a sect of New York Jews present themselves provides an example:

> Obgehitene Yiden, *"Guardian Jews,"* include those so-called ultra-Orthodox Jews who not only observe the *Shulhan Aruch* in the most minute detail but are most meticulous and zealous in their observance. They perform all the prescribed commandments and precepts with the greatest care. These people are overtly identifiable as Jews. They wear beards and/or special traditional clothing for the exclusive purpose of being externally identified as Jewish: beards so that the "image of God should be upon their faces," traditional garments so that they "may refrain from any possible sin." [115]

Stigma symbols have the character of being continuously available for perception. Some less rigid means of disclosure are also used. Fleeting offerings of evidence may be made—purposeful slips, as it were—as when a blind person voluntarily commits a clumsy act in the presence of newcomers as a way of informing them about his stigma.[116] There is also "disclosure etiquette," a formula whereby the individual admits his own failing in a matter of fact way, supporting the assumption that those present are above such concerns while preventing them from trapping themselves into showing that they are not. Thus, the "good" Jew or mental patient waits for "an appropriate time" in a conversation with strangers and calmly says: "Well, being Jewish has made me feel that . . ." or "Having had firsthand experience as a mental patient, I can . . ."

Earlier it was suggested that learning to pass constitutes one phase in the socialization of the stigmatized person and a turning point in his moral career. I want to suggest now that the stigmatized individual can come to feel that he should be above passing, that if he accepts himself and respects himself he will feel no need to conceal his failing. After laboriously learning to conceal, then,

---

[115] S. Poll, *The Hasidic Community of Williamsburg* (New York: Free Press of Glencoe, Inc., 1962), pp. 25-26.
[116] Bigman, *op. cit.*, p. 143.

the individual may go on to unlearn this concealment. It is here that voluntary disclosure fits into the moral career, a sign of one of its phases. It should be added that in the published autobiographies of stigmatized individuals, this phase in the moral career is typically described as the final, mature, well-adjusted one—a state of grace I will attempt to consider later.

Covering

A sharp distinction has been drawn between the situation of the discredited with tension to manage and the situation of the discreditable with information to manage. The stigmatized employ an adaptive technique, however, which requires the student to bring together these two possibilities. The difference between visibility and obtrusiveness is involved.

It is a fact that persons who are ready to admit possession of a stigma (in many cases because it is known about or immediately apparent) may nonetheless make a great effort to keep the stigma from looming large. The individual's object is to reduce tension, that is, to make it easier for himself and the others to withdraw covert attention from the stigma, and to sustain spontaneous involvement in the official content of the interaction. However, the means employed for this task are quite similar to those employed in passing—and in some cases identical, since what will conceal a stigma from unknowing persons may also ease matters for those in the know. It is thus that a girl who gets around best on her wooden peg employs crutches or an artful but patently artificial limb when in company.[117] This process will be referred to as *covering*. Many of those who rarely try to pass, routinely try to cover.

One type of covering involves the individual in a concern over the standards incidentally associated with his stigma. Thus the blind, who sometimes have a facial disfigurement in the region of the eyes, distinguish among themselves according to whether this is the case or not. Dark glasses sometimes worn to give volun-

[117] Baker, *op. cit.*, p. 193.

tary evidence of blindness may at the same time be worn to cover evidence of defacement—a case of revealing unsightedness while concealing unsightliness:

> The blind, in all conscience, have enough advertisement of their condition without adding a cosmetic factor to it. I can think of nothing that would add so much to the tragedy of a blind man's position as the feeling that, in the fight to regain his vision, he had lost not only the fight but the wholesomeness of his appearance as well.[118]

Similarly, since blindness can lead to the appearance of clumsiness, there may occur a special effort to re-learn motor propriety, an "ease and grace and adeptness at all those motions which the sighted world looks upon as 'normal.'" [119]

A related type of covering involves an effort to restrict the display of those failings most centrally identified with the stigma. For example, a near-blind person who knows that the persons present know about his differentness may yet hesitate to read, because to do this he would have to bring the book up to a few inches of his eyes, and this he may feel expresses too glaringly the qualities of blindness.[120] This type of covering, it should be noted, is an important aspect of the "assimilative" techniques employed by members of minority ethnic groups; the intent behind devices such as change in name and change in nose shape is not solely to pass, but also to restrict the way in which a known-about attribute obtrudes itself into the center of attention, for obtrusiveness increases the difficulty of maintaining easeful inattention regarding the stigma.

The most interesting expression of covering, perhaps, is that associated with the organization of social situations. As already suggested, anything which interferes directly with the etiquette and mechanics of communication obtrudes itself constantly into the interaction and is difficult to disattend genuinely. Hence individuals with a stigma, especially those with a physical handi-

---
[118] Chevigny, *op. cit.*, pp. 40-41.
[119] *Ibid.*, p. 123.
[120] Criddle, *op. cit.*, p. 47.

cap, may have to learn about the structure of interaction in order to learn about the lines along which they must reconstitute their conduct if they are to minimize the obtrusiveness of their stigma. From their efforts, then, one can learn about features of interaction that might otherwise be too much taken for granted to be noted.

For example, the hard of hearing learn to talk with the degree of loudness that listeners feel is appropriate for the situation, and also to be ready to deal with those junctures during interaction that specifically require good hearing if the proprieties are to be maintained:

> Frances figured out elaborate techniques to cope with "dinner lulls," intermissions at concerts, football games, dances, and so on, in order to protect her secret. But they served only to make her more uncertain, and in turn more cautious, and in turn more uncertain. Thus, Frances had it down pat that at a dinner party she should (1) sit next to someone with a strong voice; (2) choke, cough, or get hiccups, if someone asked her a direct question; (3) take hold of the conversation herself, ask someone to tell a story she had already heard, ask questions the answers to which she already knew.[121]

Similarly, the blind sometimes learn to look directly at the speaker even though this looking accomplishes no seeing, for it prevents the blind from staring off into space or hanging the head or otherwise unknowingly violating the code regarding attention cues through which spoken interaction is organized.[122]

[121] Condensed from Warfield, *Cotton in My Ears, op. cit.*, p. 36, in Wright, *op. cit.*, p. 49.
[122] Chevigny, *op. cit.*, p. 51.

3. GROUP ALIGNMENT and EGO IDENTITY

In this essay an attempt has been made to distinguish between social and personal identity. Both types of identity can be better understood by bracketing them together and contrasting them to what Erikson and others have called "ego" or "felt" identity, namely, the subjective sense of his own situation and his own continuity and character that an individual comes to obtain as a result of his various social experiences.[1]

Social and personal identity are part, first of all, of other persons' concerns and definitions regarding the individual whose

[1] The term "self identity" would be apt here but its extension, the term "self identification," is commonly used to refer to something else, namely the individual himself establishing his personal identity through documentation or testament.

identity is in question. In the case of personal identity, these concerns and definitions can arise even before he is born and continue after he has been buried, existing, then, at times when the individual himself can have no feelings at all, let alone feelings of identity. On the other hand, ego identity is first of all a subjective, reflexive matter that necessarily must be felt by the individual whose identity is at issue.[2] Thus, when a criminal uses an alias he is detaching himself from his personal identity; when he retains the original initials or some other aspect of his original name, he is at the same time indulging a sense of his ego identity.[3] Of course, the individual constructs his image of himself out of the same materials from which others first construct a social and personal identification of him, but he exercises important liberties in regard to what he fashions.[4]

The concept of social identity allowed us to consider stigmatization. The concept of personal identity allowed us to consider the role of information control in stigma management. The idea of ego identity allows us to consider what the individual may feel about stigma and its management, and leads us to give special attention to the advice he is given regarding these matters.

Ambivalence

Given that the stigmatized individual in our society acquires identity standards which he applies to himself in spite of failing to conform to them, it is inevitable that he will feel some ambivalence about his own self. Some expressions of this ambivalence have already been described in connection with the

---

[2] The three-fold typology of identity employed in this essay leaves unspecified the phrase, "to identify with," which itself has two common meanings: to participate vicariously in the situation of someone whose plight has caught one's sympathy; to incorporate aspects of another in forming one's own ego identity. The phrase, "to be identified with" can have these psychological meanings but in addition refer to the social category of persons whose presumed character is attributed to oneself as part of one's social identity.

[3] Hartman, *op. cit.*, pp. 54-55.

[4] There is, for example, a well-known tendency for a person to self-rate the prestige of his occupation higher than do those who are otherwise employed.

oscillations of identification and association the individual exhibits regarding his fellow-stigmatized. Other expressions can be cited.

The stigmatized individual exhibits a tendency to stratify his "own" according to the degree to which their stigma is apparent and obtrusive. He can then take up in regard to those who are more evidently stigmatized than himself the attitudes the normals take to him. Thus do the hard of hearing stoutly see themselves as anything but deaf persons, and those with defective vision, anything but blind.[5] It is in his affiliation with, or separation from, his more evidently stigmatized fellows, that the individual's oscillation of identification is most sharply marked.

Linked with this self-betraying kind of stratification is the issue of social alliances, namely, whether the individual's choice of friends, dates, and spouse will be held to his own group or occur "across the line." A blind girl expresses the matter:

> Once—a few years ago—I thought that I would much rather go out with a sighted man than with a blind man. But I have dates off and on, and slowly my feelings about this have changed. I value the understanding of the blind for the blind, and now I could respect a blind man for his own qualities and be glad for the understanding he could give to me.[6]
>
> Some of my friends are sighted and some are blind. This, somehow, seems to me the way it ought to be—I cannot understand regulating human relations one way or another.[7]

Presumably the more allied the individual is with normals, the more he will see himself in non-stigmatic terms, although there are contexts in which the opposite seems true.

Whether closely allied with his own kind or not, the stigmatized individual may exhibit identity ambivalence when he obtains a close sight of his own kind behaving in a stereotyped way, flamboyantly or pitifully acting out the negative attributes

[5] For example, see Criddle, *op. cit.*, pp. 44-47.
[6] Henrich and Kriegel, *op. cit.*, p. 187.
[7] *Ibid.*, p. 188.

imputed to them. The sight may repel him, since after all he supports the norms of the wider society, but his social and psychological identification with these offenders holds him to what repels him, transforming repulsion into shame, and then transforming ashamedness itself into something of which he is ashamed. In brief, he can neither embrace his group nor let it go.[8] (The phrase "concern with in-group purification" is used to describe the efforts of stigmatized persons not only to "normify" their own conduct but also to clean up the conduct of others in the group.)[9] This ambivalence seems to be found most acutely in the process of "nearing," that is, of the individual's coming close to an undesirable instance of his own kind while "with" a normal.[10]

It is only to be expected that this identity ambivalence will receive organized expression in the written, talked, acted, and otherwise presented materials of representatives of the group. Thus, in the published and stage-performed humor of the stigmatized is to be found a special kind of irony. Cartoons, jokes, and folk tales display unseriously the weaknesses of a stereotypical member of the category, even while this half-hero is made to guilelessly outwit a normal of imposing status.[11] The serious presentations of the representatives can exhibit a similar ambivalence, telling of a similar self-alienation.

Professional Presentations

It has been suggested that the stigmatized individual defines himself as no different from any other human being, while at the same time he and those around him define him as

---

[8] See J.-P. Sartre, *Anti-Semite and Jew* (New York: Grove Press, 1960), pp. 102 ff.
[9] M. Seeman, "The Intellectual and the Language of Minorities," *American Journal of Sociology*, LXIV (1958), 29.
[10] An interesting episode in which a near-blind youth meets a blind girl at a charity booth and has mixed responses is recorded in Criddle, *op. cit.*, pp. 71-74.
[11] See, for example, J. Burma, "Humor as a Technique in Race Conflict," *American Sociological Review*, XI (1946), 710-715.

someone set apart. Given this basic self-contradiction of the stigmatized individual it is understandable that he will make some effort to find a way out of his dilemma, if only to find a doctrine which makes consistent sense out of his situation. In contemporary society, this means that the individual will not only attempt on his own to hammer out such a code, but that, as already suggested, professionals will help out—sometimes in the guise of telling their life story or of telling how they handled a difficult situation.

The codes that are presented to the stigmatized individual, whether explicitly or implicitly, tend to cover certain standard matters. A desirable pattern of revealing and concealing is suggested. (For example, in the case of the ex-mental patient it is sometimes recommended that he properly conceal his stigma from mere acquaintances but feel secure enough in his sanity, and believe enough in the medical, not moral, nature of his past failings, to reveal himself to his spouse, his close friends, and his employer.) Other standard matters are: formulae for dealing with ticklish situations; the support he should give to his own; the type of fraternization with normals that should be maintained; the kinds of prejudice against his own kind that he should blink at and the kinds he should openly attack; the extent to which he should present himself as a person as normal as anyone else, and the extent to which he should encourage his receiving slightly different treatment; the facts about his own kind he should take pride in; the "facing up to" his own differentness that he should engage in.

Although the codes or lines presented to those with a particular stigma will differ among themselves, there are certain arguments, however contradictory, that are very generally agreed on. The stigmatized person is almost always warned against attempting to pass completely. (After all, except for the anonymous confessor, it might be difficult for anyone to advocate this tack in open print.) Too, he is generally warned against fully accepting as his own the negative attitudes of others toward him. He is likely to be warned against "minstrelization," [12] whereby the stigmatized person ingratiatingly acts out before normals the full dance of bad qualities imputed to his kind, thereby consolidating a life situation into a clownish role:

> I also learned that the cripple must be careful not to act differently from what people expect him to do. Above all they expect the cripple to be crippled; to be disabled and helpless: to be inferior to themselves, and they will become suspicious and insecure if the cripple falls short of these expectations. It is rather strange, but the cripple has to play the part of the cripple, just as many women have to be what the men expect them to be, just women; and the Negroes often have to act like clowns in front of the "superior" white race, so that the white man shall not be frightened by his black brother.
>
> I once knew a dwarf who was a very pathetic example of this, indeed. She was very small, about four feet tall, and she was extremely well educated. In front of people, however, she was very careful not to be anything other than "the dwarf," and she played the part of the fool with the same mocking laughter and the same quick, funny movements that have been the characteristics of fools ever since the royal courts of the Middle Ages. Only when she was among friends, she could throw away her cap and bells and dare to be the woman she really was: intelligent, sad, and very lonely.[13]

And, contrariwise, he is usually warned against "normification" or "deminstrelization";[14] he is encouraged to have distaste for those of his fellows who, without actually making a secret of their stigma, engage in careful covering, being very careful to show that in spite of appearances they are very sane, very generous, very sober, very masculine, very capable of hard physical labor and taxing sports, in short, that they are gentlemen de-

---

[12] The term comes from A. Broyard, "Portrait of the Inauthentic Negro," *Commentary*, X (1950), 59-60. A conscious effort at fully playing the role is involved, sometimes termed "impersonation." On Negroes impersonating Negroes, see Wolfe, *op. cit.*, p. 203.

[13] Carling, *op. cit.*, pp. 54-55.

[14] Lewin, *op. cit.*, pp. 192-193, uses the term "negative chauvinism" here; Broyard, *op. cit.*, p. 62, uses the term "role inversion." See also Sartre, *op. cit.*, pp. 102 ff.

viants, nice persons like ourselves in spite of the reputation of their kind.[15]

It should be plain that these advocated codes of conduct provide the stigmatized individual not merely with a platform and a politics, and not merely with instruction as to how to treat others, but with recipes for an appropriate attitude regarding the self. To fail to adhere to the code is to be a self-deluded, misguided person; to succeed is to be both real and worthy, two spiritual qualities that combine to produce what is called "authenticity."[16]

Two implications of this advocacy might be mentioned here. First, this advice about personal conduct sometimes stimulates the stigmatized individual into becoming a critic of the social scene, an observer of human relations. He may be led into placing brackets around a spate of casual social interaction so as to examine what is contained therein for general themes. He can become "situation conscious" while normals present are spontaneously involved *within* the situation, the situation itself constituting for these normals a background of unattended matters. This extension of consciousness on the part of the stigmatized persons is reinforced, as earlier suggested, by his special aliveness to the contingencies of acceptance and disclosure, contingencies to which normals will be less alive.[17]

---

[15] On Jews, see Sartre, *op. cit.*, pp. 95-96; on Negroes, see Broyard, *op. cit.*; on intellectuals, see M. Seeman, *op. cit.*; on the Japanese, see M. Grodzins, "Making Un-Americans," *American Journal of Sociology*, LX (1955), 570-582.

[16] It should be noted that although the literature on authenticity is concerned with how the individual ought to behave, and is therefore moralistic, nonetheless it is presented in the guise of dispassionate neutral analysis, since authenticity is supposed to imply a realistic reality-orientation; and in fact at this time this literature is the best source of neutral analysis concerning these identity issues. For critical comments, see I. D. Rinder and D. T. Campbell, "Varieties of Inauthenticity," *Phylon*, Fourth Quarter, 1952, 270-275.

[17] This is merely one aspect of the general tendency for stigmatized individuals to face a wide review and capsulation of their life, where a normal might not have to. Thus, a stigmatized person who obtains a family and job is sometimes said to have "made something out of his life." Similarly, someone who marries a stigmatized person is said to have "thrown his life away." All this is reinforced in some cases by the individual becoming a "case" for social workers or other welfare officers and retaining this case status for the remainder of his life. On the attitude of one blind person to this, see Chevigny, *op. cit.*, p. 100.

Secondly, advice to the stigmatized often deals quite candidly with the part of his life that he feels is most private and shameful; his most deeply hidden sores are touched on and examined in the clinical manner that is a current literary fashion.[18] Intense debates regarding personal positions can be presented in fictionalized form, along with thorough-going crises of conscience. Fantasies of humiliation and of triumph over normals can be packaged and made available. Here the most private and embarrassing is the most collective, for the stigmatized individual's deepest feelings are made of just the stuff that verbal and vocal members of his category present in a well-rounded version. And since what is available to the stigmatized is necessarily available to us, these presentations can hardly avoid raising the issue of exposure and betrayal, even though their ultimate effect is probably helpful to the situation of the stigmatized.

In-Group Alignments

Although these proposed philosophies of life, these recipes of being, are presented as though from the stigmatized individual's personal point of view, on analysis it is apparent that something else informs them. This something else is groups, in the broad sense of like-situated individuals, and this is only to be expected, since what an individual is, or could be, derives from the place of his kind in the social structure.

One of these groups is the aggregate formed by the individual's fellow-sufferers. The spokesmen of this group claim that the individual's real group, the one to which he *naturally* belongs, is this group.[19] All the other categories and groups to which the individual necessarily also belongs are implicitly considered to be

[18] The recent writings of James Baldwin provide good material of this kind in regard to Negroes. Chevigny's *My Eyes Have a Cold Nose* provides a good example in regard to the blind.

[19] Hence, for example, Lewin, *op. cit.*, can discuss the phenomenon he calls self-hate and cause no confusion even though he means by the term not the individual's hate for himself (which Lewin sees as a frequent result of self-hate), but hate for the group to which the individual's stigma consigns him.

not his real ones; he is not really one of them. The individual's real group, then, is the aggregate of persons who are likely to have to suffer the same deprivations as he suffers because of having the same stigma; his real "group," in fact, is the category which can serve as his discrediting.

The character these spokesmen allow the individual is generated by the relation he has to those of his own kind. If he turns to his group, he is loyal and authentic; if he turns away, he is craven and a fool.[20] Here, surely, is a clear illustration of a basic sociological theme: the nature of an individual, as he himself and we impute it to him, is generated by the nature of his group affiliations.

As might be expected, professionals who take an in-group standpoint may advocate a militant and chauvinistic line—even to the extent of favoring a secessionist ideology. Taking this tack, the stigmatized individual in mixed contacts will give praise to the assumed special values and contributions of his kind. He may also flaunt some stereotypical attributes which he could easily cover; thus, one finds second generation Jews who

---

[20] The admonition that the stigmatized individual should be loyal to his group is voiced by professional social scientists, too. For example, Riesman, in "Marginality, Conformity, and Insight," *Phylon*, Third Quarter, 1953, 251-252, in describing how a sociologist, or an American, or a professor may each be seduced into accepting compliments regarding his self that are an insult to his group, adds this story:

I myself recall that I once told a woman lawyer that she was not as strident and aggressive as other Portias I had known, and I regret that she took this as a compliment and consented to the betrayal of her female colleagues of the bar.

Sociologically, it should be clear that in finding himself in different social situations, the individual will find himself facing different claims as to which of his many groups is his real one. Other matters are less clear. Why, for example, should individuals who have already paid a considerable price for their stigma be told not to pass; perhaps according to the rule that the less you've had the less you should try to obtain? And if derogation of those with a particular stigma is bad in the present and bad for the future, why should those who have the stigma, *more so than those who don't*, be given the responsibility of presenting and enforcing a fair-minded stand and improving the lot of the category as a whole? One answer, of course, is that those with the stigma should "know better," thus assuming an interesting relation between knowledge and morality. A better answer, perhaps, is that those with a particular stigma are often considered by themselves and by normals to be linked together through space and time into a single community that should be supported by its members.

aggressively interlard their speech with Jewish idiom and accent, and the militant gay who are patriotically swish in public places. The stigmatized individual may also openly question the half-concealed disapproval with which normals treat him, and wait to "fault" the self-appointed wise, that is, continue to examine the others' actions and words until some fugitive sign is obtained that their show of accepting him is only a show.[21]

The problems associated with militancy are well known. When the ultimate political objective is to remove stigma from the differentness, the individual may find that his very efforts can politicize his own life, rendering it even more different from the normal life initially denied him—even though the next generation of his fellows may greatly profit from his efforts by being more accepted. Further, in drawing attention to the situation of his own kind he is in some respects consolidating a public image of his differentness as a real thing and of his fellow-stigmatized as constituting a real group. On the other hand, if he seeks some kind of separateness, not assimilation, he may find that he is necessarily presenting his militant efforts in the language and style of his enemies. Moreover, the pleas he presents, the plight he reviews, the strategies he advocates, are all part of an idiom of expression and feeling that belongs to the whole society. His disdain for a society that rejects him can be understood only in terms of that society's conception of pride, dignity, and independence. In short, unless there is some alien culture on which to fall back, the more he separates himself structurally from the normals, the more like them he may become culturally.

Out-Group Alignments

The individual's "own" group, then, may inform the code of conduct professionals advocate for him. The stigmatized individual is also asked to see himself from the point of view of a

[21] On the militant response of some patients with facial deformities, see Macgregor et al., op. cit., p. 84. See also, C. Greenberg, "Self-Hatred and Jewish Chauvinism," *Commentary*, X (1950), 426-433.

GROUP ALIGNMENT AND EGO IDENTITY

second grouping: the normals and the wider society that they constitute. I want to consider at some length the shadow cast by this second standpoint.

The language of this stance inspired by normals is not so much political, as in the previous case, as it is psychiatric—the imagery of mental hygiene being employed as a source of rhetoric. He who adheres to the advocated line is said to be mature and to have achieved a good personal adjustment; he who does not follow the line is said to be an impaired person, rigid, defensive, with inadequate inner resources. What does this advocacy involve?

The individual is advised to see himself as a fully human being like anyone else, one who at worst happens to be excluded from what is, in the last analysis, merely one area of social life. He is not a type or a category, but a human being:

> Who said that cripples are unfortunate? Do they, or do you? Just because they can't dance? All music has to stop sometime anyway. Just because they can't play tennis? Lots of times the sun is too hot! Just because you have to help them up and down stairs? Is there something else you would rather do? Polio is not sad—it is just darned inconvenient—it means you can't have those fits of temper and run into your room and kick the door shut any more. *Cripples* is an awful word. It specifies! It sets apart! It is too intimate! It is condescending! It makes me want to vomit like a wiggling creature coming out of the cocoon.[22]

Since his affliction is nothing in itself, he should not be ashamed of it or of others who have it; nor should he compromise himself by trying to conceal it. On the other hand, by hard work and persistent self-training he should fulfill ordinary standards as fully as he can, stopping short only when the issue of normification arises; that is, where his efforts might give the impression that he is trying to deny his differentness. (This very fine line is drawn differently, of course, by different professionals, but because of this ambiguity it needs professional presentation all the

[22] Linduska, *op. cit.*, pp. 164-165.

more.) And because normals have their troubles, too, the stigmatized individual should not feel bitter, resentful, or self-pitying. A cheerful, outgoing manner should be cultivated.

A formula for handling normals follows logically. The skills that the stigmatized individual acquires in dealing with a mixed social situation should be used to help the others in it.

Normals really mean no harm; when they do, it is because they don't know better. They should therefore be tactfully helped to act nicely. Slights, snubs, and untactful remarks should not be answered in kind. Either no notice should be taken or the stigmatized individual should make an effort at sympathetic re-education of the normal, showing him, point for point, quietly, and with delicacy, that in spite of appearances the stigmatized individual is, underneath it all, a fully-human being. (So complete is the individual's derivation from society, that society can rely on those who are the least accepted as normal members, the least rewarded by the pleasures of easy social intercourse with others, to provide a statement, clarification, and tribute to the inward being of everyman. The more the stigmatized individual deviates from the norm, the more wonderfully he may have to express possession of the standard subjective self if he is to convince others that he possesses it, and the more they may demand that he provide them with a model of what an ordinary person is supposed to feel about himself.)

When the stigmatized person finds that normals have difficulty in ignoring his failing, he should try to help them and the social situation by conscious efforts to reduce tension.[23] In these circumstances the stigmatized individual may, for example, attempt to "break the ice," explicitly referring to his failing in a way that shows he is detached, able to take his condition in stride. In addition to matter-of-factness, levity is also recommended:

> Then there was the cigarette gag. That was invariably good for a laugh. Whenever I'd walk into a restaurant, bar, or party I'd whip

[23] An attempt is made to provide a general analysis of this type of tension and its reduction in E. Goffman, "Fun in Games," in *Encounters* (New York: Bobbs-Merrill, 1961), especially pp. 48-55.

out a pack of butts, open it ostentatiously, take one, light it, and sit back puffing on it contentedly. That almost always attracted attention. People would stare and I could almost hear them saying, My! Isn't it wonderful what he can do with a pair of hooks? Whenever anyone commented on this accomplishment I'd smile and say, "There's one thing I never have to worry about. That's burning my fingers." Corny, I know, but a sure icebreaker . . .[24]

A somewhat sophisticated female patient whose face had been scarred by a beauty treatment felt it effective upon entering a room of people to say facetiously, "Please excuse the case of leprosy."[25]

It is also suggested that the stigmatized individual in mixed company may find it useful to refer to his disability and his group in the language he employs when with his own, and the language employed about him when normals are among their own—thus proffering the normals present a temporary status as wise ones. At other times he may find it appropriate to conform to "disclosure etiquette" and introduce his failing as a topic of serious conversation, in this way hoping to reduce its significance as a topic of suppressed concern:

[24] Russell, *op. cit.*, p. 167, in Wright, *op. cit.*, p. 177; see also Russell, *op. cit.*, p. 151. It should be noted that he who attempts to break the ice may, of course, be seen as exploiting the situation for what can be wrung from it, as novelists have pointed out. I. Levin, *A Kiss Before Dying* (New York: Simon and Schuster, 1953), pp. 178-179, provides an example:

> *"Oh yes," Kingship said, "he's poor all right. He took pains to mention it exactly three times the other night. And that anecdote he dragged in, about the woman his mother did sewing for."*
> *"What's wrong with his mother taking in sewing?"*
> *"Nothing, Marion, nothing. It's the way he alluded to it so casually, so very casually. Do you know who he reminded me of? There's a man at the club who has a bad leg, limps a little. Every time we play golf he says, 'You boys go on ahead. Old Peg-leg'll catch up with you.' So everyone walks extra slowly and you feel like a heel if you beat him."*

And in being able to break the ice, he may be demonstrating to himself that he has superior control in the situation (Henrich and Kriegel, *op. cit.*, p. 145):

> *I think it is not the responsibility of society to understand the cerebral palsied, but rather it is our duty to tolerate society and, in the name of chivalry, forgive and be amused by its folly. I find it a dubious honor, but challenging and entertaining. Putting obviously disturbed or curious people at ease before they have a chance to complicate a situation places the handicapped in a role superior to that of the agitators and adds to the human comedy. But this is something it takes a very long time to learn.*

[25] Macgregor et al., *op. cit.*, p. 85.

> The injured man's feeling that, *as a person*, he is not understood, combined with the non-injured person's embarrassment in his presence, produces a strained, uncomfortable relationship which further serves to separate them. To relieve this social strain and gain greater acceptance, the injured person may not only be willing to satisfy the expressed curiosity of non-injured persons ... but may also himself initiate discussion of the injury ...[26]

Other means of helping the others to be tactful toward him are also recommended, such as, in the case of facial disfigurements, pausing on the threshold of an encounter so the participants-to-be will have a chance to compose their response.

> A 37-year-old male whose face is grossly disfigured but who carries on a real estate business stated, "When I have an appointment with a new contact, I try to manage to be standing at a distance and facing the door, so the person entering will have more time to see me and get adjusted to my appearance before we start talking."[27]

The stigmatized individual is also advised to act as if the efforts of normals to ease matters for him were effective and appreciated. Unsolicited offers of interest, sympathy, and help, although often perceived by the stigmatized as an encroachment on privacy and a presumption, are to be tactfully accepted:

> Yet, help is not only a problem to those who render it. If the cripple wants the ice to be broken, he must admit the value of help and allow people to give it to him. Innumerable times I have seen the fear and bewilderment in people's eyes vanish as I have stretched out my hand for help, and I have felt life and warmth stream from the helping hands I have taken. We are not always aware of the help we may give by accepting aid, that in this way we may establish a foothold for contact.[28]

A polio patient author states a similar theme:

[26] White, Wright, and Dembo, *op. cit.*, pp. 16-17.
[27] Macgregor *et al.*, *op. cit.*, p. 85.
[28] Carling, *op. cit.*, pp. 67-68.

> When my neighbors ring my bell on a snowy day to inquire if I need something from the store, even though I am prepared for bad weather I try to think up some item rather than reject a generous offer. It is kinder to accept help than refuse it in an effort to prove independence.[29]

And similarly, an amputee:

> A lot of amputees sort of humor the others to make them feel good because they are doing something for you. It doesn't make other people uncomfortable like it could if you were still standing up.[30]

Although the tactful acceptance of clumsy efforts by others to help may be a burden to the stigmatized individual, more is asked of him. It is said that if he is really at ease with his differentness, this acceptance will have an immediate effect upon normals, making it easier for them to be at ease with him in social situations. In brief, the stigmatized individual is advised to accept himself as a normal person because of what others can gain in this way, and hence likely he himself, during face-to-face interaction.

The line inspired by normals, then, obliges the stigmatized individual to protect normals in various ways. An important aspect of this protection has only been suggested; it will be reconsidered here.

Given the fact that normals in many situations extend a stigmatized person the courtesy of treating his defect as if it were of no concern, and that the stigmatized is likely to feel that underneath it all he is a normal human being like anyone else, the stigmatized can be expected to allow himself sometimes to be taken in and to believe that he is more accepted than he is. He will then attempt to participate socially in areas of contact which others feel are not his proper place. Thus a blind writer describes the consternation he caused in a hotel barber shop:

---

[29] Henrich and Kriegel, *op. cit.*, p. 185.
[30] G. Ladieu, E. Hanfmann, and T. Dembo, "Evaluation of Help by the Injured," *Journal of Abnormal and Social Psychology*, XLII (1947), 182.

The shop was hushed and solemn as I was ushered in and I was virtually lifted by the uniformed attendant into the chair. I tried a joke, the usual thing about getting a haircut once every three months even if I didn't need it. It was a mistake. The silence told me that I wasn't a man who should make jokes, not even good ones.[31]

Similarly in regard to dancing:

People seemed a little shocked to hear about it. I had spent an afternoon tea dancing at the Savoy Plaza. They couldn't explain why they had their feeling, and my announcement that I had enjoyed it hugely and intended to do it again at the first opportunity seemed to make things worse. It was all just something a blind man shouldn't be up to. . . . It has the general flavor of not properly observing one's period of mourning.[32]

A cripple adds another illustration:

But people do not only expect you to play your part; they also expect you to know your place. I remember for instance a man at an open-air restaurant in Oslo. He was much disabled, and he had left his wheel-chair to ascend a rather steep staircase up to the terrace where the tables were. Because he could not use his legs he had to crawl on his knees, and as he began to ascend the stairs in this unconventional way, the waiters rushed to meet him, not to help, but to tell him that they could not serve a man like him at that restaurant, as people visited it to enjoy themselves and have a good time, not to be depressed by the sight of cripples.[33]

That the stigmatized individual can be caught taking the tactful acceptance of himself too seriously indicates that this acceptance is conditional. It depends upon normals not being pressed past the point at which they can easily extend acceptance—or, at worst, uneasily extend it. The stigmatized are tact-

---

[31] Chevigny, *op. cit.*, p. 68.
[32] *Ibid.*, p. 130.
[33] Carling, *op. cit.*, p. 56

fully expected to be gentlemanly and not to press their luck; they should not test the limits of the acceptance shown them, nor make it the basis for still further demands. Tolerance, of course, is usually part of a bargain.

The nature of a "good adjustment" is now apparent. It requires that the stigmatized individual cheerfully and unselfconsciously accept himself as essentially the same as normals, while at the same time he voluntarily withholds himself from those situations in which normals would find it difficult to give lip service to their similar acceptance of him.

Since the good-adjustment line is presented by those who take the standpoint of the wider society, one should ask what the following of it by the stigmatized means to normals. It means that the unfairness and pain of having to carry a stigma will never be presented to them; it means that normals will not have to admit to themselves how limited their tactfulness and tolerance is; and it means that normals can remain relatively uncontaminated by intimate contact with the stigmatized, relatively unthreatened in their identity beliefs. It is from just these meanings, in fact, that the specifications of a good adjustment derive.

When a stigmatized person employs this stance of good adjustment he is often said to have a strong character or a deep philosophy of life, perhaps because in the back of our minds we normals want to find an explanation of his willingness and ability to act this way. A blind person's statement may be cited:

> The disbelief that one's desire to go on can spring from quite ordinary motives is so generally encountered that as a defense against it you almost automatically develop a rationale to explain your behavior. You develop a "philosophy." People seem to insist that you have one and they think you're kidding when you say you haven't. So you do your best to please and to strangers you encounter on trains, in restaurants, or on the subway who want to know what keeps you going, you give your little piece. You're a man of unusual discernment if you can realize that your philosophy is

seldom one of your own devising but a reflection of the world's notion about blindness.[34]

The general formula is apparent. The stigmatized individual is asked to act so as to imply neither that his burden is heavy nor that bearing it has made him different from us; at the same time he must keep himself at that remove from us which ensures our painlessly being able to confirm this belief about him. Put differently, he is advised to reciprocate naturally with an acceptance of himself and us, an acceptance of him that we have not quite extended him in the first place. A *phantom acceptance* is thus allowed to provide the base for a *phantom normalcy*. So deeply, then, must he be caught up in the attitude to the self that is defined as normal in our society, so thoroughly must he be a part of this definition, that he can perform this self in a faultless manner to an edgy audience that is half-watching him in terms of another show. He can even be led to join with normals in suggesting to the discontented among his own that the slights they sense are imagined slights—which of course is likely at times, because at many social boundaries the markers are designed to be so faint as to allow everyone to proceed as though fully accepted, and this means that it will be realistic to be oriented to minimal signs perhaps not meant.

The irony of these recommendations is not that the stigmatized individual is asked to be patiently for others what they decline to let him be for them, but that this expropriation of his response may well be the best return he can get on his money. If in fact he desires to live as much as possible "like any other person," and be accepted "for what he really is," then in many cases the shrewdest position for him to take is this one which has a false bottom; for in many cases the degree to which normals accept the stigmatized individual can be maximized by his acting with full spontaneity and naturalness as if the conditional acceptance

[34] Chevigny, *op. cit.*, pp. 141-142. The writer goes on to suggest that this philosophy may even be demanded of persons born blind and hence not in a very good position to learn what it is they have successfully compensated for.

of him, which he is careful not to overreach, is full acceptance. But of course what is a good adjustment for the individual can be an even better one for society. It might be added that the embarrassment of limits is a general feature of social organization; the maintenance of phantom acceptance is what many, to some degree, are being asked to accept. Any mutual adjustment and mutual approval between two individuals can be fundamentally embarrassed if one of the partners accepts in full the offer that the other appears to make; every "positive" relationship is conducted under implied promises of consideration and aid such that the relationship would be injured were these credits actually drawn on.

The Politics of Identity

The in-group and the out-group, then, both present an ego identity for the stigmatized individual, the first largely in political phrasings, the second in psychiatric ones. The individual is told that if he adopts the right line (which line depending on who is talking), he will have come to terms with himself and be a whole man; he will be an adult with dignity and self-respect.

And in truth he will have accepted a self for himself; but this self is, as it necessarily must be, a resident alien, a voice of the group that speaks for and through him.

But all of us, sociology sometimes claims, speak from the point of view of a group. The special situation of the stigmatized is that society tells him he is a member of the wider group, which means he is a normal human being, but that he is also "different" in some degree, and that it would be foolish to deny this difference. This differentness itself of course derives from society, for ordinarily before a difference can matter much it must be conceptualized collectively by the society as a whole. This can be clearly seen in the case of our newly-instituted stigmas, as a person with one of them suggests:

Having been born an athetoid type of cerebral palsy as the result of a birth injury to the control center of the brain, I was not aware of my startling, complex classification until the term became popular and society insisted that I admit my labeled deviations. It was something like joining Alcoholics Anonymous. You cannot be honest with yourself until you find out what you are and, perhaps, consider what society thinks you are or should be.[35]

This is even more clear in the case of epilepsy. Since Hippocrates' time, those who discover they have this disorder have been assured a firmly stigmatized self by the definitional workings of society. This work still goes on even though insignificant physical impairment may be involved, and even though many medical specialists now use the term to refer to a seizure disorder only when no specific (and less stigmatizing) medical disorder can be found.[36] Here the point where medical science must withdraw is the point where society can act most determinatively.

Thus, even while the stigmatized individual is told that he is a human being like everyone else, he is being told that it would be unwise to pass or to let down "his" group. In brief, he is told he is like anyone else and that he isn't—although there is little agreement among spokesmen as to how much of each he should claim to be. This contradiction and joke is his fate and his destiny. It constantly challenges those who represent the stigmatized, urging these professionals to present a coherent politics of identity, allowing them to be quick to see the "inauthentic" aspects of other recommended programs but slow indeed to see that there may be no "authentic" solution at all.

The stigmatized individual thus finds himself in an arena of detailed argument and discussion concerning what he ought to think of himself, that is, his ego identity. To his other troubles he must add that of being simultaneously pushed in several directions by professionals who tell him what he should do and feel about what he is and isn't, and all this purportedly in his

[35] Henrich and Kriegel, *op. cit.*, p. 155.
[36] Livingston, *op. cit.*, p. 5 and pp. 291-304.

own interests. To write or give speeches advocating any one of these "avenues of flight" is an interesting solution in itself, but one that is denied, alas, to most of those who merely read and listen.

4. THE SELF and ITS OTHER

This essay deals with the situation of the stigmatized person and his response to the spot he is in. In order to place the resulting framework in its proper conceptual context, it will be useful to consider from different angles the concept of deviation, this being a bridge which links the study of stigma to the study of the rest of the social world.

Deviations and Norms

It is possible to think of rare and dramatic failings as those most suitable for the analysis here employed. However, it would seem that exotic differentness is most useful merely as a means of making one aware of identity assumptions ordinarily so fully satisfied as to escape one's awareness. It is also possible to think that established minority groups like Negroes and Jews can provide the best objects for this kind of analysis. This could easily lead to imbalance of treatment. Sociologically, the central issue concerning these groups is their place in the social structure; the contingencies these persons encounter in face-to-face interaction is only one part of the problem, and something that cannot itself be fully understood without reference to the history, the political development, and the current policies of the group.

It is also possible to restrict the analysis to those who possess a flaw that uneases almost all their social situations, leading these unfortunates to form a major part of their self-conception reactively, in terms of their response to this plight.[1] This report argues differently. The most fortunate of normals is likely to have his half-hidden failing, and for every little failing there is a social occasion when it will loom large, creating a shameful gap between virtual and actual social identity. Therefore the occasionally precarious and the constantly precarious form a single continuum, their situation in life analyzable by the same framework. (Hence persons with only a minor differentness find they understand the structure of the situation in which the fully stigmatized are placed—often attributing this sympathy to the profundity of their human nature instead of to the isomorphism of human situations. The fully and visibly stigmatized, in turn, must suffer the special indignity of knowing that they wear their situation on their sleeve, that almost anyone will be able to see into the heart of their predicament.) It is implied, then, that it is not to the different that one should look for understanding our differentness, but to the ordinary. The question of social norms is certainly central, but the concern might be less for uncommon deviations from the ordinary than for ordinary deviations from the common.

It can be assumed that a necessary condition for social life is the sharing of a single set of normative expectations by all par-

[1] What Lemert, *Social Pathology, op. cit.*, pp. 75 ff., has titled "secondary deviance."

ticipants, the norms being sustained in part because of being incorporated. When a rule is broken restorative measures will occur; the damaging is terminated and the damage repaired, whether by control agencies or by the culprit himself.

However, the norms dealt with in this paper concern identity or being, and are therefore of a special kind. Failure or success at maintaining such norms has a very direct effect on the psychological integrity of the individual. At the same time, mere desire to abide by the norm—mere good will—is not enough, for in many cases the individual has no immediate control over his level of sustaining the norm. It is a question of the individual's condition, not his will; it is a question of conformance, not compliance. Only by introducing the assumption that the individual should know and keep his place can a full equivalent in willful action be found for the individual's social condition.

Further, while some of these norms, such as sightedness and literacy, may be commonly sustained with complete adequacy by most persons in the society, there are other norms, such as those associated with physical comeliness, which take the form of ideals and constitute standards against which almost everyone falls short at some stage in his life. And even where widely attained norms are involved, their multiplicity has the effect of disqualifying many persons. For example, in an important sense there is only one complete unblushing male in America: a young, married, white, urban, northern, heterosexual Protestant father of college education, fully employed, of good complexion, weight, and height, and a recent record in sports. Every American male tends to look out upon the world from this perspective, this constituting one sense in which one can speak of a common value system in America. Any male who fails to qualify in any of these ways is likely to view himself—during moments at least—as unworthy, incomplete, and inferior; at times he is likely to pass and at times he is likely to find himself being apologetic or aggressive concerning known-about aspects of himself he knows are probably seen as undesirable. The general identity-values of a society may be fully entrenched nowhere, and yet they can cast some kind of shadow on the encounters encountered everywhere in daily living.

Moreover, more is involved than norms regarding somewhat static status attributes. The issue is not merely visibility but obtrusiveness; this means that failure to sustain the many minor norms important in the etiquette of face-to-face communication can have a very pervasive effect upon the defaulter's acceptability in social situations.

Therefore it is not very useful to tabulate the numbers of persons who suffer the human predicament outlined in this book. As Lemert once suggested, the number would be as high as one wanted to make it;[2] and when those with a courtesy stigma are added, and those who once experienced the situation or are destined, if for no other reason than oncoming agedness, to do so, the issue becomes not whether a person has experience with a stigma of his own, because he has, but rather how many varieties he has had his own experience with.

One can say, then, that identity norms breed deviations as well as conformance. Two general solutions to this normative predicament were cited earlier. One solution was for a category of persons to support a norm but be defined by themselves and others as not the relevant category to realize the norm and personally to put it into practice. A second solution was for the individual who cannot maintain an identity norm to alienate himself from the community which upholds the norm, or refrain from developing an attachment to the community in the first place. This is of course a costly solution both for society and for the individual, even if it is one that occurs in small amounts all the time.

The processes detailed here constitute together a third main solution to the problem of unsustained norms. Through these processes the common ground of norms can be sustained far beyond the circle of those who fully realize them; this is a statement, of course, about the social function of these processes and

---

[2] E. Lemert, "Some Aspects of a General Theory of Sociopathic Behavior," *Proceedings of the Pacific Sociological Society*, State College of Washington, XVI (1948), 23-24.

not about their cause or their desirability. Passing and covering are involved, providing the student with a special application of the arts of impression management, the arts, basic in social life, through which the individual exerts strategic control over the image of himself and his products that others glean from him. Also involved is a form of tacit cooperation between normals and the stigmatized: the deviator can afford to remain attached to the norm because others are careful to respect his secret, pass lightly over its disclosure, or disattend evidence which prevents a secret from being made of it; these others, in turn, can afford to extend this tactfulness because the stigmatized will voluntarily refrain from pushing claims for acceptance much past the point normals find comfortable.

The Normal Deviant

It should be seen, then, that stigma management is a general feature of society, a process occurring wherever there are identity norms. The same features are involved whether a major differentness is at question, of the kind traditionally defined as stigmatic, or a picayune differentness, of which the shamed person is ashamed to be ashamed. One can therefore suspect that the role of normal and the role of stigmatized are parts of the same complex, cuts from the same standard cloth. Of course, psychiatrically oriented students have often pointed out the pathological consequence of self-derogation, just as they have argued that prejudice against a stigmatized group can be a form of sickness. These extremes, however, have not concerned us, for the patterns of response and adaptation considered in this essay seem totally understandable within a framework of normal psychology. One can assume first that persons with different stigmas are in an appreciably similar situation and respond in an appreciably similar way. The neighborly druggist might talk to the neighborhood, therefore neighborhood drugstores have been avoided by persons seeking all manner of equipment and medication—persons wonderfully diverse who share nothing but a need to control information. And secondly, one can assume that the stigmatized and the normal have the same mental make-up, and that this necessarily is the standard one in our society; he who can play one of these roles, then, has exactly the required equipment for playing out the other, and in fact in regard to one stigma or another is likely to have developed some experience in doing so. Most important of all, the very notion of *shameful* differences assumes a similarity in regard to crucial beliefs, those regarding identity. Even where an individual has quite abnormal feelings and beliefs, he is likely to have quite normal concerns and employ quite normal strategies in attempting to conceal these abnormalities from others, as the situation of ex-mental patients suggests:

> One of the difficulties centers around the meaning of "reasonable employment." The patients are sometimes unable, but more often unwilling, to explain why a particular job is "unreasonable" or impossible for them. One middle-aged man could not bring himself to explain that he was so terrified of the dark that he insisted on sharing his bedroom with his aunt, and that he could not possibly work where it meant coming home alone in the dark in winter. He tries to overcome his fear, but is reduced to a state of physical collapse if left alone at night. In such an instance—and there were many others—the ex-patient's fears of ridicule, contempt or harshness make it difficult for him to explain the real reason for refusing or not holding the jobs offered to him. He may then easily be labelled as work-shy or unemployable, which is likely to be financially disastrous.[8]

Similarly, when an aging person finds he cannot remember the names of some of his immediate friends, he may shy away from going to the meeting places where he is likely to encounter them, thus illustrating an embarrassment and a plan which entail human capacities that have nothing to do with aging.

If, then, the stigmatized person is to be called a deviant, he might better be called a *normal deviant*, at least to the extent that

[8] Mills, *op. cit.*, p. 105.

his situation is analyzed within the framework presented here.

There is direct evidence regarding this self-other, normal-stigmatized unity. For example, it seems that persons who suddenly find themselves relieved of a stigma, as in successful plastic surgery, may quickly be seen, by themselves and others, to have altered their personality, an alteration in the direction of the acceptable,[4] just as those who have suddenly acquired a defect may relatively quickly experience a change in apparent personality.[5] These perceived changes seem to be a result of the individual's being placed in a new relationship to the contingencies of acceptance in face-to-face interaction, with consequent employment of new strategies of adaptation. Important additional evidence comes from social experiments, wherein subjects knowingly take on a defect (temporarily, of course), such as partial deafness, and find themselves spontaneously manifesting the reactions and employing the devices that are found among the actually handicapped.[6]

A further fact should be mentioned. Because a change from stigmatized status to normal status is presumably in a desired direction, it is understandable that the change, when it comes, can be sustained psychologically by the individual. But it is very difficult to understand how individuals who sustain a sudden transformation of their life from that of a normal to that of a stigmatized person can survive the change psychologically; yet very often they do. That both types of transformation can be sustained—but especially the latter type—suggests that standard capacities and training equip us to handle both possibilities. And once these possibilities are learned, the rest, alas, comes easily. For the individual to learn that he is beyond the pale, or not beyond the pale after having been beyond, is not, then, a complicated thing, merely a new alignment within an old frame of reference, and a taking to himself in detail what he had known about before as residing in others. The painfulness, then, of

[4] Macgregor *et al.*, *op. cit.*, pp. 126-129.
[5] *Ibid.*, pp. 110-114.
[6] L. Meyerson, "Experimental Injury: An Approach to the Dynamics of Physical Disability," *Journal of Social Issues*, IV (1948), 68-71. See also Griffin, *op. cit.*

sudden stigmatization can come not from the individual's confusion about his identity, but from his knowing too well what he has become.

Taken through time, then, the individual is able to play both parts in the normal-deviant drama. But one must see that even boxed within a brief social moment, the individual may be able to perform both shows, exhibiting not only a general capacity to sustain both roles, but also the detailed learning and command necessary for currently executing the required role behavior. This is facilitated, of course, by the fact that the roles of stigmatized and normal are not merely complementary; they also exhibit some striking parallels and similarities. Performers of each role may withdraw from contact with the other as a means of adjustment; each may feel that he is not fully accepted by the other; each may feel that his own conduct is being watched too closely—and be correct in this feeling. Each may stay with his "own" merely to forgo having to face the problem. Further, the asymmetries or differences between the roles that do exist are often kept within such limits as will further the common and crucial task of maintaining the social situation that is in progress. Aliveness to the role of the other must be sufficient so that when certain adaptive tactics are not employed by one of the normal-stigmatized pair, the other will know how to step in and take on the role. For example, should the stigmatized person fail to present his failing in a matter of fact way, the normal may assume the task. And when normals try tactfully to help the stigmatized person with his difficulties, he may grit his teeth and accept help gracefully, out of regard for the good will of the effort.

Evidence of two-headed role playing is widely available. For example, whether for fun or seriously, people pass, and they do so in both directions, into or out of the stigmatized category. Another source of evidence is psychodrama. This "therapy" assumes that mental patients and others beyond the pale can on stage switch parts and play out the role of normal to someone who is now playing their role to them; and in fact they can perform this theater without much prompting and with reasonable competency. A third source of evidence that the individual can simultaneously sustain command over both the normal and stigmatized role comes to us from behind-scenes joshing. Normals, when among themselves, "take off" on a stigmatized type. More to the point, the stigmatized in similar circumstances takes off on the normal as well as himself. He jokingly enacts scenes of degradation with one of his kind playing the role of the crudest of normals while he affects the complementary role for a moment, only to break into vicarious rebelliousness. As part of this sad pleasure there will be the unserious use of stigma terms of address that are usually tabooed in "mixed" society.[7] It should be restated here that this kind of joking by the stigmatized does not so much demonstrate some kind of chronic distance the individual has from himself as it demonstrates the more important fact that a stigmatized person is first of all like anyone else, trained first of all in others' views of persons like himself, and differing from them first of all in having a special reason to resist stigma derogation when in their presence and the special license to give voice to it when in their absence.

A special case of the light use of self-abusing language and style is provided by professional representatives of the group. When representing their group to normals, they may embody in an exemplary way the ideals of the normal, being partly chosen for being able to do so. However, when attending social affairs among their own, they may feel a special obligation to show that they have not forgotten about the ways of the group or their own place, and so on stage may employ native dialect, gesture, and expression in humorous caricature of their identity. (The audience can then dissociate themselves from what they still have a little of, and identify with what they haven't yet fully

[7] For example, in regard to Negroes, see Johnson, *op. cit.*, p. 92. On the use of "crazy" by mental patients see, for example, I. Belknap, *Human Problems of a State Mental Hospital* (New York: McGraw-Hill Book Company, 1956), p. 196; and J. Kerkhoff, *How Thin the Veil* (New York: Greenberg, 1952), p. 152. Davis, "Deviance Disavowal," *op. cit.*, pp. 130-131, provides examples in regard to the physically handicapped, pointing out that use of these terms with normals will be a sign that the normals are wise.

become.) These performances, however, often have a cultivated, trim aspect; something has been clearly placed in brackets and raised to an art. In any case, one regularly finds in the same representative the capacity to be more "normal" in manner than are most of the members of his category who orient themselves in this direction, while at the same time he can command more of the native idiom than those of his category who are oriented in this direction. And where a representative doesn't have this capacity to manage two faces, he will find himself under some pressure to develop it.

Stigma and Reality

Until now it has been argued that a central role should be given to discrepancies between virtual and actual social identity. Tension management and information management have been stressed—how the stigmatized individual can present to others a precarious self, subject to abuse and discrediting. But to leave it at this creates a biased perspective, imputing solid reality to what is much shakier than that. The stigmatized and the normal are part of each other; if one can prove vulnerable, it must be expected that the other can, too. For in imputing identities to individuals, discreditable or not, the wider social setting and its inhabitants have in a way compromised themselves; they have set themselves up to be proven the fool.

All of this has already been implied in the statement that passing is sometimes done for what is seen as fun. The person who very occasionally passes often recounts the incident to his fellows as evidence of the foolishness of the normals and the fact that all their arguments about his differentness from them are merely rationalizations.[8] These errors of identification are chuckled over, gloated over by the passer and his friends. Similarly one finds that those who at the moment are routinely concealing their personal or occupational identity may take pleasure in tempting the devil, in bringing a conversation with

[8] See Goffman, *Asylums, op. cit.,* p. 112.

unsuspecting normals around to where the normals are unknowingly led to make fools of themselves by expressing notions which the presence of the passer quite discredits. In such cases what has proven false is not the person with a differentness, but rather any and all those who happen into the situation and there attempt to sustain conventional patterns of treatment.

But there are of course even more direct instances of the situation, not the person, becoming threatened. The physically handicapped, for example, in having to receive overtures of sympathy and inquiry from strangers, may sometimes protect their privacy by exercising something other than tact. Thus, a one-legged girl, prone to many inquiries by strangers concerning her loss, developed a game she called "Ham and Legs" in which the play was to answer an inquiry with a dramatically presented preposterous explanation.[9] A different girl with the same plight reports a similar strategy:

> Questions about how I lost my leg used to annoy me, so I developed a stock answer that kept these people from asking further: "I borrowed some money from a loan company and they are holding my leg for security!" [10]

Brief responses that terminate the unwanted encounter are also reported:

> "My poor girl, I see you've lost your leg."
> That's the opportunity for the *touché*, "How careless of me!" [11]

In addition, there is the much less gentle art of "putting the other on," whereby militant members of disadvantaged groups, during sociable occasions, build up a story, about themselves and their feelings, to normals who clumsily profess sympathy, the story reaching a point where it becomes patent that the story was designed to reveal itself to be a fabrication.

[9] Baker, *op. cit.*, pp. 92-94.
[10] Henrich and Kriegel, *op. cit.*, p. 50.
[11] Baker, *op. cit.*, p. 97, in Wright, *op. cit.*, p. 212.

A cold stare, of course, may forestall an encounter before it has been initiated, as illustrated from the memoirs of an aggressive dwarf:

> There were the thick-skinned ones, who stared like hill people come down to see a travelling show. There were the paper-peekers, the furtive kind who would withdraw blushing if you caught them at it. There were the pitying ones, whose tongue clickings could almost be heard after they had passed you. But even worse, there were the chatterers, whose every remark might as well have been "How do you do, poor boy?" They said it with their eyes and their manners and their tone of voice.
>
> I had a standard defense—a cold stare. Thus anesthetized against my fellow man, I could contend with the basic problem—getting in and out of the subway alive.[12]

From here it is only one step to crippled children who manage occasionally to beat up someone who taunts them, or persons, politely but clearly excluded from certain settings, politely and clearly entering the settings in numbers and with determination.[13]

The social reality sustained by the tractable member of a particular stigmatized category and the normal with civility will itself have a history. When, as in the case of divorce or Irish ethnicity, an attribute loses much of its force as a stigma, a period will have been witnessed when the previous definition of the situation is more and more attacked, first, perhaps, on the comedy stage, and later during mixed contacts in public places, until it ceases to exert control over both what can be easefully attended, and what must be kept a secret or painfully disattended.

In conclusion, may I repeat that stigma involves not so much a set of concrete individuals who can be separated into two piles,

---

[12] Viscardi, *A Man's Stature*, p. 70, in Wright, *op. cit.*, p. 214. On similar techniques employed by a man with hooks, see Russell, *op. cit.*, pp. 122-123.

[13] An experiment along these lines is recorded in M. Kohn and R. Williams, Jr., "Situational Patterning in Intergroup Relations," *American Sociological Review*, XXI (1956), 164-174.

the stigmatized and the normal, as a pervasive two-role social process in which every individual participates in both roles, at least in some connections and in some phases of life. The normal and the stigmatized are not persons but rather perspectives. These are generated in social situations during mixed contacts by virtue of the unrealized norms that are likely to play upon the encounter. The lifelong attributes of a particular individual may cause him to be type-cast; he may have to play the stigmatized role in almost all of his social situations, making it natural to refer to him, as I have done, as a stigmatized person whose life-situation places him in opposition to normals. However, his particular stigmatizing attributes do not determine the nature of the two roles, normal and stigmatized, merely the frequency of his playing a particular one of them. And since interaction roles are involved, not concrete individuals, it should come as no surprise that in many cases he who is stigmatized in one regard nicely exhibits all the normal prejudices held toward those who are stigmatized in another regard.

Now certainly it seems that face-to-face interaction, at least in American society, is constructed in such a way as to be particularly prone to the kind of trouble considered in this essay. It also seems that discrepancies between virtual and actual identity will always occur and always give rise to the need for tension management (in regard to the discredited), and information control (in regard to the discreditable). And where stigmas are very visible or intrusive, or are transmissible along family lines, then the resulting instabilities in interaction can have a very pervasive effect upon those accorded the stigmatized role. However, the perceived undesirability of a *particular* personal property, and its capacity to trigger off these stigma-normal processes, has a history of its own, a history that is regularly changed by purposeful social action. And although it can be argued that the stigma processes seem to have a general social function—that of enlisting support for society among those who aren't supported by it—and to that degree presumably are resistant to change, it must be seen that additional functions seem to be involved which vary markedly according to the type of stigma. The stigmatization of those with a bad moral record clearly can function as a means of formal social control; the stigmatization of those in certain racial, religious, and ethnic groups has apparently functioned as a means of removing these minorities from various avenues of competition; and the devaluation of those with bodily disfigurements can perhaps be interpreted as contributing to a needed narrowing of courtship decisions.[14]

[14] For this latter suggestion, I am grateful to David Matza.

5. DEVIATIONS and DEVIANCE

Once the dynamics of shameful differentness are seen as a general feature of social life, one can go on to look at the relation of their study to the study of neighboring matters associated with the term "deviance"—a currently fashionable word that has been somewhat avoided here until now, in spite of the convenience of the label.[1]

Starting with the very general notion of a group of individuals

[1] It is remarkable that those who live around the social sciences have so quickly become comfortable in using the term "deviant," as if those to whom the term is applied have enough in common so that significant things can be said about them as a whole. Just as there are iatrogenic disorders caused by the work that physicians do (which then gives them more work to do), so there are categories of persons who are created by students of society, and then studied by them.

who share some values and adhere to a set of social norms regarding conduct and regarding personal attributes, one can refer to any individual member who does not adhere to the norms as a deviator, and to his peculiarity as a deviation. I do not think all deviators have enough in common to warrant a special analysis; they differ in many more ways than they are similar, in part because of the thorough difference, due to size, of groups in which deviations can occur. One can, however, subdivide the area into smaller plots, some of which might be worth cultivating.

It is known that a confirmed high position in some small close-knit groups can be associated with a license to deviate and hence to be a deviator. The relation of such a deviator to the group, and the conception members have of him, are such as to withstand restructuring by virtue of the deviation. (When the group is large, however, the eminent may find they must fully conform in all visible ways.) The member who is defined as physically sick is in somewhat the same situation; if he properly handles his sick status he can deviate from performance standards without this being taken as a reflection on him or on his relation to the group. The eminent and the sick can be free, then, to be deviators precisely because their deviation can be fully discounted, leading to no re-identification; their special situation demonstrates they are anything but deviants—in the common understanding of that term.[2]

In many close-knit groups and communities there are instances of a member who deviates, whether in deed or in the attributes he possesses, or both, and in consequence comes to play a special role, becoming a symbol of the group and a performer of certain clownish functions, even while he is denied the respect accorded full-fledged members.[3] Characteristically this individual ceases to play the social distance game, approaching and being approached at will. He is often the focus of attention

---

[2] The complex relation of a deviator to his group has recently been reconsidered by L. Coser, "Some Functions of Deviant Behavior and Normative Flexibility," *American Journal of Sociology*, LXVIII (1962), 172-181.

[3] On these and other functions of the deviant, see R. Dentler and K. Erickson, "The Functions of Deviance in Groups," *Social Problems*, VII (1959), 98-107.

that welds others into a participating circle around him, even while it strips him of some of the status of a participant. He serves as a mascot for the group although qualified in certain ways to be a normal member of it. The village idiot, the small-town drunk, and the platoon clown are traditional examples; the fraternity fat boy is another. One would expect to find only one of such persons to a group, since one is all that is needed, further instances merely adding to the burden of the community. He might be called an *in-group deviant* to remind one that he is deviant relative to a concrete group, not merely norms, and that his intensive if ambivalent inclusion in the group distinguishes him from another well-known type of deviator—the group isolate who is constantly in social situations with the group but is not one of their own. (When the in-group deviant is attacked by outsiders, the group may well rally in support; when the group isolate is attacked, he is more likely to have to do his own fighting.) Note that all the types of deviators considered here are fixed within a circle in which extensive biographical information about them—a full personal identification—is widespread.

It has been suggested that in smallish groups the in-group deviant can be distinguished from other deviators, for unlike these others he is in a skewed relation to the moral life that is sustained on the average by the members. Indeed, if one did want to consider other social roles along with the in-group deviant, it might be useful to turn to those roles whose performers are out of step with ordinary morality, although not known as deviators. As one shifts the "system of reference" from small family-like groups to ones which can support greater role specialization, two such roles become evident. One of these morally mis-aligning roles is that of minister or priest, the performer being obliged to symbolize the righteous life and live it more than is normal; the other is that of law officer, the performer having to make a daily routine out of other people's appreciable infractions.[4]

---

[4] This theme is developed in H. Becker, *Outsiders* (New York: Free Press of Glencoe, 1963), pp. 145-163.

DEVIATIONS AND DEVIANCE

When the "system of reference" is further shifted from a face-to-face local community to the wider world of metropolitan settlements (and their affiliated areas, resort and residential), a corresponding shift is found in the variety and meaning of deviations.

One such deviation is important here, the kind presented by individuals who are seen as declining voluntarily and openly to accept the social place accorded them, and who act irregularly and somewhat rebelliously in connection with our basic institutions[5]—the family, the age-grade system, the stereotyped role-division between the sexes, legitimate full-time employment involving maintenance of a single governmentally ratified personal identity, and segregation by class and race. These are the "disaffiliates." Those who take this stand on their own and by themselves might be called eccentrics or "characters." Those whose activity is collective and focused within some building or place (and often upon a special activity) may be called cultists. Those who come together into a sub-community or milieu may be called *social deviants*, and their corporate life a deviant community.[6] They constitute a special type, but only one type, of deviator.

If there is to be a field of inquiry called "deviance," it is social deviants as here defined that would presumably constitute its core. Prostitutes, drug addicts, delinquents, criminals, jazz musicians, bohemians, gypsies, carnival workers, hobos, winos, show people, full time gamblers, beach dwellers, homosexuals,[7]

[5] A general point suggested to me by Dorothy Smith.
[6] The term "deviant community" is not entirely satisfactory because it obscures two issues: whether or not the community is peculiar according to structural standards derived from an anlysis of the make-up of ordinary communities; and whether or not the members of the community are social deviants. A one-sexed army post in an unpopulated territory is a deviant community in the first sense, but not necessarily a community of social deviants.
[7] The term "homosexual" is generally used to refer to anyone who engages in overt sexual practices with a member of his own sex, the practice being called "homosexuality." This usage appears to be based on a medical and legal frame of reference and provides much too broad and heterogeneous a categorization for use here. I refer only to individuals who participate in a special community of understanding wherein members of one's own sex are defined as the most desirable sexual objects, and sociability is energetically organized around the pursuit and entertain-

and the urban unrepentant poor—these would be included. These are the folk who are considered to be engaged in some kind of collective denial of the social order. They are perceived as failing to use available opportunity for advancement in the various approved runways of society; they show open disrespect for their betters; they lack piety; they represent failures in the motivational schemes of society.

Once the core of social deviancy is established, one can proceed to peripheral instances: community-based political radicals who not only vote in a divergent way but spend more time with those of their own kind than is politically necessary; the traveling rich who are not geared into the executive's work week, and spend their time drifting from one summering place to another; expatriates, employed or not, who routinely wander at least a few steps from the PX and the American Express; the ethnic assimilation backsliders who are reared in the two worlds of the parent society and the society of their parents, and resolutely turn away from the conventional routes of mobility open to them, overlaying their public school socialization with what many normals will see as a grotesque costume of religious orthodoxy; the metropolitan unmarried and merely married who disavail themselves of an opportunity to raise a family, and instead support a vague society that is in rebellion, albeit mild and short-lived, against the family system. In almost all of these cases, some show of disaffiliation is made, as is also true of eccentrics and cultists, providing in this way a thin line that can be drawn between all of them and deviators on the other side, namely, the quietly disaffiliated—hobbyists who become so devoted to their avocation

---

ment of these objects. According to this conception there are four basic varieties of homosexual life: the male and the female types found in custodial institutions; and the male and female "gay" worlds sustained in urban centers. (In this latter connection, see E. Hooker, *op. cit.*) Note that an individual can retain membership in the gay world and yet not engage in homosexual practices, just as he can exploit the gay through sale of sexual favors without participating socially and spiritually in the gay community. (In this latter connection see Reiss, *op. cit.*) If the term homosexual is used to refer to someone who engages in a particular kind of sexual act, then a term like "homosexualite" is needed to refer to someone who participates in a particular kind of deviant community.

that only a husk remains for civil attachments, as in the case of some ardent stamp collectors, club tennis players, and sports car buffs.

Social deviants, as defined, flaunt their refusal to accept their place and are temporarily tolerated in this gestural rebellion, providing it is restricted within the ecological boundaries of their community. Like ethnic and racial ghettos, these communities constitute a haven of self-defense and a place where the individual deviator can openly take the line that he is at least as good as anyone else. But in addition, social deviants often feel that they are not merely equal to but better than normals, and that the life they lead is better than that lived by the persons they would otherwise be. Social deviants also provide models of being for restless normals, obtaining not only sympathy but also recruits. (Cultists acquire converts too, of course, but the focus is on programs of action not styles of life.) The wise can become fellow-travelers.

In theory, a deviant community could come to perform for society at large something of the same functions performed by an in-group deviant for his group, but while this is thinkable, no one yet seems to have demonstrated the case. The problem is that the large area from which recruits to a deviant community are drawn is not itself as clearly a system, an entity, with needs and functions, as is a small face-to-face group.

Two kinds of deviators have been here considered: in-group deviants and social deviants. Two neighboring types of social category ought to be mentioned. First, ethnic and racial minority groups:[8] individuals who have a common history and culture (and often a common national origin), who transmit their membership along lineage lines, who are in a position to demand signs of loyalty from some of the members, and who are in a relatively disadvantaged position in society. Secondly, there are those members of the lower class who quite noticeably bear the mark of their status in their speech, appearance, and manner,

[8] For a recent analytical treatment, see R. Glass, "Insiders-Outsiders: The Position of Minorities," *New Left Review*, XVII (Winter, 1962), 34-45.

and who, relative to the public institutions of our society, find they are second class citizens.

Now it is apparent that in-group deviants, social deviants, minority members, and lower class persons are all likely on occasion to find themselves functioning as stigmatized individuals, unsure of the reception awaiting them in face-to-face interaction and deeply involved in the various responses to this plight. This will be so if for no other reason than that almost all adults have to have some dealings with service organizations, both commercial and civil, where courteous, uniform treatment is supposed to prevail based on nothing more restrictive than citizenship, but where opportunity will arise for concern about invidious expressive valuations based on a virtual middle class ideal.

It should be just as apparent, however, that a full consideration of any one of these four categories leads beyond, and away from, what it is necessary to consider in the analysis of stigma. For example, there are deviant communities whose members, especially when away from their milieux, are not particularly concerned about their social acceptance, and therefore can hardly be analyzed by reference to stigma management; an instance would be certain outdoor milieux on the warm beaches of America where can be found those aging young people who are not yet ready to become contaminated by work and who voluntarily devote themselves to various forms of riding the waves. Nor should it be forgotten that apart from the four categories mentioned, there are some disadvantaged persons who are not stigmatized at all, for example, someone married to a mean and selfish mate, or someone who is not well off and must raise four children,[9] or someone whose physical handicap (for example, a mild hearing disability) has interfered with his life, even though everyone, including himself, remains unaware that he has a physical disability.[10]

I have argued that stigmatized persons have enough of their

---
[9] Toynbee, *op. cit.*, Chaps. 15 and 17.
[10] An instance is to be found in Henrich and Kriegel, *op. cit.*, pp. 178-180.

situations in life in common to warrant classifying all these persons together for purposes of analysis. An extraction has thus been made from the traditional fields of social problems, race and ethnic relations, social disorganization, criminology, social pathology, and deviancy—an extraction of something all these fields have in common. These commonalities can be organized on the basis of very few assumptions regarding human nature. What remains in each one of the traditional fields could then be re-examined for whatever is really special to it, thereby bringing analytical coherence to what is now purely historic and fortuitous unity. Knowing what fields like race relations, aging, and mental health share, one could then go on to see, analytically, how they differ. Perhaps in each case the choice would be to retain the old substantive areas, but at least it would be clear that each is merely an area to which one should apply several perspectives, and that the development of any one of these coherent analytic perspectives is not likely to come from those who restrict their interest exclusively to one substantive area.

ABOUT THE AUTHOR

Erving Goffman was born in Manville, Alberta (Canada) in 1922. He came to the United States in 1945, and in 1953 received his Ph.D. in sociology from the University of Chicago. He was professor of sociology at the University of California at Berkeley until 1968, and thereafter was Benjamin Franklin Professor of Anthropology and Sociology at the University of Pennsylvania in Philadelphia. Dr. Goffman received the MacIver Award in 1961 and the In Medias Res Award in 1978. He was a Fellow of the American Academy of Arts and Sciences. He died in 1983.

Dr. Goffman's books include *The Presentation of Self in Everyday Life, Encounters, Asylums, Behavior in Public Places, Stigma, Interaction Ritual, Strategic Interaction, Relations in Public, Frame Analysis,* and *Gender Advertisements.*

Outstanding Books from the Touchstone Library

☐ **Man's Search for Meaning: An Introduction to Logotherapy**
by Viktor E. Frankl
One of the world's preeminent psychiatrists describes an affirmative, existential psychotherapy born out of his experiences in Nazi death camps. "Perhaps the most significant thinking since Freud and Adler."—*The American Journal of Psychiatry*
0-671-24422-1 $9.00

☐ **Mortal Lessons: Notes on the Art of Surgery**
by Richard Selzer, M.D.
A surgeon's essays on the human body, mind, and spirit. "A beautiful book . . . Dr. Selzer's vision and words are poetic."—Edmund Fuller, *The Wall Street Journal*
0-671-64102-6 $8.95

☐ **Transformations: Growth and Change in Adult Life**
by Roger L. Gould, M.D.
Based on exhaustive research, Dr. Gould's book reveals that most adult crises are age-related and follow predictable patterns. "A unique, profound, and exciting discovery."—*Psychotherapy and Social Science Review*
0-671-25066-3 $12.95

☐ **Death: The Final Stage of Growth**
by Elisabeth Kübler-Ross
Dr. Kübler-Ross, the world-renowned psychiatrist whose pioneering work identified the five stages of terminal illness, shows how we come to terms with the idea of death. "Immensely valuable and satisfying."
Library Journal
0-671-62238-2 $9.00

☐ **The Road Less Traveled: A New Psychology of Love, Traditional Values, and Spiritual Growth**
by M. Scott Peck, M.D.
A psychiatrist's best-selling synthesis of psychological and spiritual insights. "A spontaneous act of generosity."—Phyllis Theroux, *The Washington Post*
0-671-25067-1 $12.00

------ MAIL COUPON TODAY—NO-RISK 14-DAY FREE TRIAL ------

Simon & Schuster Inc.
200 Old Tappan Road, Customer Order Department
Old Tappan, NJ 07675

Please send me copies of the books checked above.
(If not completely satisfied, you may return for full refund within 14 days.)
☐ Save! Enclose full amount per *copy* with this coupon (publisher pays postage and handling) or put charge on your credit card.
☐ Master Card   ☐ Visa
My credit card number is _____ Card expires _____

Signature _____

Name _____
(Please Print)

Address _____

City _____ State _____ Zip Code _____
or available at your local bookstore   Prices subject to change without notice